GOOGLE ADVERTISING A-Z
ESSENTIAL ADWORDS & IMAGE ADS TIPS FOR GETTING THE MOST CLICKS AT THE L

Second E

ISBN: 0-976

C000127009

By

Editors of BottleTree Books LLC

www.BottleTreeBooks.com

GOOGLE ADVERTISING A-Z
ESSENTIAL ADWORDS & IMAGE ADS TIPS FOR GETTING THE MOST CLICKS
AT THE LOWEST COST

Second Edition
ISBN: 0-9762541-5-8

TM

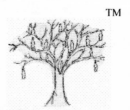

BottleTreeBooks.com

BottleTree Books LLC publishes literary fiction and Internet topic books. Its staff of publishing and Internet professionals includes an intellectual property attorney with university majors in computer engineering and electrical engineering.

Also from BottleTree

OVERTURE & YAHOO ADVERTISING
PLUS 110 TIPS & TRICKS

ISBN: 097625414X

Do you want to learn the ins and outs of Overture and Yahoo advertising to make your products and services available for up to 275 million searches per day? Do you want to take advantage of 110 tips and tricks to dominate selling on Overture and Yahoo? Whether you are new to Pay-Per-Click advertising or a seasoned marketer, *Overture and Yahoo Advertising* will show you how in a quick and easy format loaded with charts, guides, hyperlinks to free Internet advertising tools, tables and 110 tips and tricks to maximizing your Return-on-Investment. See why a successful advertising campaign on Overture and Yahoo is much different than one on Google.

Here is but a sampling of the topics covered:
- ➢ Bid traps – How to exploit and avoid them
- ➢ Get free Overture coupons worth $25 to $50
- ➢ How to get a Premium Listing without bidding in the top 3 spots
- ➢ The Yahoo Premium Listing exception
- ➢ Secrets of Content Match
- ➢ The CNN Premium Listing exception
- ➢ How to list your business for free on Yahoo's Local Match
- ➢ Examples of great ad titles
- ➢ The best keyword placement within the Bodylines
- ➢ Definitive ad stylization
- ➢ Tricks to keyword plurals and misspellings
- ➢ Guide to Overture foreign countries and languages
- ➢ 25 examples of ads that work on Yahoo and those that don't
- ➢ Commonly overlooked Yahoo advertising programs
- ➢ How to budget and control your monthly spending
- ➢ And a much more. . .

Google Advertising A-Z
Essential AdWords & Image Ads Tips for Getting the Most Clicks at the Lowest Cost

Second Edition
ISBN: 0-9762541-5-8

A first edition of "Google Advertising A-Z: Essential AdWords & Image Ads Tips for Getting the Most Clicks at the Lowest Cost" was published under ISBN: 0976254107 in October 2004. © Copyright BottleTree Books LLC. All Rights Reserved.

TM

*Nothing in this publication is to be construed as legal advice or counseling.

TABLE OF CONTENTS

I.   Introduction

A. The Huge Business Potential of Google Advertising

Google is one of the most widely used search engines. It gains 60 million unique viewers per month with over 200 million searches conducted per day. This results in over 8 million searches per hour, 140 thousand searches each minute or over 2000 searches each *second* by people and businesses hungry to buy your products and services. Google is also one of the most comprehensive search engines. It reviews over 8 billion Websites for each query to return the most relevant results. The potential to increase your business using Google advertising is huge. Signing up is easy and it takes only a few minutes. Once your credit or debit card information has been inputted and your ads created, they begin showing on Google in a matter of minutes! The advertising opportunities are limitless and Google has developed two revolutionary ways in which you can tap these search results: AdWords and Image Ads.

B. Introduction to AdWords & Image Ads

In the right-hand column next to Google's search results AdWords are displayed – four lines of text that identify your business, products, or services and provide a link to your Website. Image Ads are graphic ads that are shown in place of AdWords text ads on Google partner sites. When users type in one of your designated search terms or "keywords," impressions of your ad are shown. You pay on a Cost-Per-Click (CPC) basis, which means you only pay when your ad is clicked on, otherwise, you are getting free advertising. AdWords and Image Ads are displayed in any Internet Explorer or Netscape browser higher than version 2.X, which means 99% of Internet users will be able to see your ad. This also includes Apple's popular Safari browser.

Title Line:	Life of Edgar Allan Poe
Bodyline1:	Historical Novel "Coffee with Poe."
Bodyline2:	His Life, Romances & Struggles!
URL Line:	AndrewBarger.com
Region:	New York

Below you'll learn how to get top placement on AdWords and Image Ads by paying a fraction of what your competitors do. You'll also learn how to make your ad stand out among the rest even if you don't get top placement. In addition, you'll discover how to launch an effective advertising campaign on Google that is finely tuned to the best keywords, which will get you not only the most click-throughs, but also the most sales. We'll demonstrate which ads work the best in 6 primary market areas. Along the way you'll be shown over 60 tips and optimization techniques for your ads. Using *Google Advertising A-Z* you'll be on your way to increased profitability at the lowest cost.

C. The Vast Reach of Google Advertising

Google has created two networks on which AdWords and Image Ads are displayed apart from the Google search page.

1. Search Network

Google has used its innovative technology to partner with some of the Internet's most widely used search engines and portals such as AOL, Excite, Ask Jeeves, etc. Not only are AdWords displayed each time one of the 200 million searches are conducted each day on Google, they are also displayed during searches on Google's partner sites. Currently, however, you are unable to select which partners show your ad in the Google Search Network.

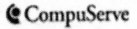 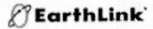

  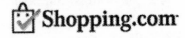

2. Content Network

Google has also compiled an impressive array of Websites on which AdWords and Image Ads are displayed when users search on specific articles. Just as in the Google Search Network, you are unable to select which partners show your ad in the Google Content Network.

The number of users clicking on your contextual ad is typically lower than the Click-Through-Rate (CTR) of search ads due to increased competition from other information on the page. The good news is that when users do click on your contextual ad, they are just as likely to buy your product, opt into your newsletter, etc as those clicking off the Google search page.

3. Gmail

In 2004 Google introduced the world to its free email program called Gmail. Under this free and evolutionary email program, Google computers scan email messages for keywords and phrases. Google inserts AdWords text alongside the email message. Gmail users then click on these ads from within their email messages to buy your products or services. This is yet another market for your Google advertising campaign.

BID IN THE TOP 3 SPOTS FOR GMAIL INCLUSION

TIP: In our tests if an email message is 20 lines or less, only the top 3 ads will be shown next to the message. What this means is that the vast majority of email messages will only show 3 ads next to them so bidding into the top 3 spots is a must to get good Gmail exposure!

4. Google Print

Google also introduced Google Print in 2004, which allows book publishers to have their books scanned into electronic format and partially displayed when a Google searcher types in a keyword or phrase contained in the book. This includes copies of old books housed in university libraries that are long out of circulation. Now, what does this mean for you as a Google advertiser? It is yet another place where your ads are displayed. When your keywords are the same as those searched on in the section of the book, your ad is displayed alongside the book results. If your ad is clicked on, Google shares the click payment with the book publisher. The great thing is this comes out of Google's pocket. You do not have to pay more for these clicks even though Google is getting less revenue.

D. The AdSense Marketing Advantage

AdSense allows AdWords and Image Ads to be displayed on individual Websites. Google has created html code that is inserted into a particular Website to easily enable this. Google searches the enabled Websites and inserts AdWords or Image Ads that would be tailored to the interests of visitors. When the ads are clicked on, Google pays the Website owner a percentage of the amount paid to Google, i.e., the CPC, just as it does for book publishers with Google Print.

amazon.com

Amazon.com is a great example. It commonly displays three advertisements when users search for books and other products. They are listed under the "Customers who are interested in this title may also be interested in:" phrase. Although not an official Google partner (Amazon has it own search engine called A9), Amazon uses Google's AdSense program to increase its revenues. When someone clicks on an ad, Amazon gets additional revenue from Google. What does this mean for you as an advertiser? In addition to your ads having the potential to be displayed during the 200 million searches conducted on Google each day, your ads are further displayed on millions of other Websites and AdSense sites, including massive Websites such as Amazon.com.

E. Low Google Advertising Costs

Now that the vast scope and reach of Google advertising have been established, let's cut right to the chase: How much will you pay to reach this kind of audience: $100, $1000, $10,000? How about 5¢? For as little as 5¢ per click and 5¢ per day you can advertise on AdWords and Image Ads. That's right, you can advertise on Google for $.05 per day. You set the amount you are willing to spend on advertising. Once customers click on your ad and have used up your max daily budget, your ad will no longer run for that day. It is that simple. You are always in control of your advertising budget and the cost barriers are nonexistent to advertise on Google.

Minimum Cost-Per-Click	Maximum Cost-Per-Click
$.05 USD	$50 USD

Google has a built-in smart pricing feature that will adjust your CPC lower on content sites if clicks there are not getting "business results." How Google defines this term is broadly. It includes revenues, email list registrations, clicks on AdSense advertisements that may be displayed on your Website, newsletter signups, etc.

The amount you pay each day can also be as little as 5¢ up to an unlimited amount. There are no monthly commitments or minimum monthly expenditures for your advertisements on Google and it only charges a $5 sign up fee.

Minimum Daily Budget	Maximum Daily Budget
$.05 USD	Unlimited

For large advertisers, Premium Sponsorship ads are displayed in the predominate window at the top of the Google search results. Anyone spending $5000 or more a month advertising with Google is eligible for Premium Sponsorship.

AdWords coupons are almost impossible to find, but we have found two exceptions to this rule that most advertisers do not know about. Strangely enough you can get a $50 Adwords coupon by signing up with Google's main advertising rival—Overture. Here's how:

SIGN UP FOR OVERTURE'S MERCHANT SOLUTIONS

$$$: With each Merchant Solution program you will receive $50 click credit on *both* Overture and Google. If you are going to register with Merchant Solutions, do it *before* signing up for Overture or Google's AdWords to get these free click credits. To sign up for Merchant Solutions, simply call 1-866-781-9246 or visit http://smallbusiness.yahoo.com/merchant.

The second way to get a free AdWords coupon is by signing up for Google's AdSense (lots of details on this groundbreaking program later). Google often runs AdSense promotions where existing AdWords customers receive free advertising money by launching AdSense for the first time on their Website. These offerings are for limited durations, so check with Google frequently.

SIGN UP FOR ADSENSE DURING PROMOTION PERIODS

$$$: Google sometimes offers $25 click credit for existing AdWords customers that sign up for AdSense and earn a minimum amount of Adsense revenue by a certain date. If you are already an AdWords customer, you do not need to do anything. Google will mail or email you about future promotions if you are not running AdSense on your Website. If you are not an AdWords customer, visit http://www.google.com/credit25 to see if a promo is running.

F. The Google Advertising Structure

Google has broken down its advertising structure into two main parts:
Campaigns, and AdGroups. Beneath these you specify the keywords
applicable to each AdGroup, the countries in which the ad will run, and
the languages in which the ad will be displayed.

Google Advertising Structure

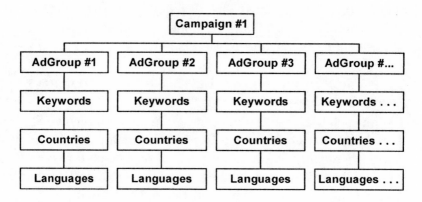

1. Campaigns

The first level in Google's advertising structure is the Campaign level.
Think of this level as a product category for your marketing strategy. If
you have an online store that sells clothes, shoes, hats and scarves, a
Campaign should be started for each of these categories.

2. AdGroups

Numerous AdGroups can be created in each Campaign. In our example
above, under the clothing campaign, separate AdGroups could be created
for "dress shirts," "long sleeve shirts," "flannel shirts," etc. within a
"shirts" campaign.

Limits on Google's Advertising Structure
1. 25 Maximum Campaigns Per Account
2. 100 Maximum AdGroups Per Campaign
3. 1000 Maximum Keywords Per AdGroup

This means you have 2.5 million variations to determine which keywords are generating the most click-throughs for your ads!

The ads shown for each AdGroup are rotated evenly and Google tracks which are performing the best by having the greatest CTR. You can then remove your poorly performing ads or tweak them for optimum CTRs.

CREATE AN AdGroup FOR EACH KEYWORD

TIP: If you are only marketing a few specific products or services, and are bidding on a handful of highly specific keywords, create an AdGroup for *each* keyword or phrase that uses that keyword or phrase in the title. Imagine the interest your ad will draw if when users type in "Handkerchiefs" they get the following tailored ad:

Handkerchiefs
1000+ Brands. Monogrammed
for free! Low Prices Guaranteed!
[Website].com

G. Build Brand Identity for Free on Google

There are no costs for people viewing your ad on Google! This is a great way to build brand identity on the Internet, which is the second highest goal of marketers right behind increased sales. Again, there are no costs for people viewing your ad on Google. You will be hard pressed to find that feature on any traditional marketing medium where advertising costs are based on the number of people hearing the ad (radio) or viewing the ad (TV, billboards, magazine articles). With Google AdWords and Image Ads the traditional scattershot way of advertising is over. You can target your ad to the exact customers needing your product or services they come to you first by searching for your products or services. This is direct-response advertising at its highest level. Google only requires at least 5 clicks per 1000 impressions of your ad. This is not much and it means that 995 potential customers could be viewing your ad free of charge. If we extrapolate the numbers, only 50 clicks are needed for 10,000 impressions, giving you 9,950 free advertisements at a minimum cost of $2.50 USD given $.05 USD per click.

II. AdWords Bid Strategies, Impression Frequency, and Position Placement

A. The Key to Getting #1 Placement on Google

At first glance Google's pay-for-performance system appears to reward those bidding the highest amount for keywords with top placement in the AdWords column. The logic follows that if one advertiser is paying $10 each time a customer searches on "cars" and clicks on its ad, while the next highest bidder is paying $2.50, the higher advertiser should receive top placement in the AdWords column. Surprisingly, this is not the case. The number of *clicks* your ad receives on Google is the most important factor to gaining top placement within the Google advertising system! This is your click-through-rate, or CTR, and it is vital to the success of your marketing campaign on Google. This simple mathematical formula is how placement is calculated:

$$\left[\frac{\text{Clicks}}{\text{1 Day}} \right]\left[\frac{\$ \text{ xx}}{\text{Clicks}} \right] = \frac{\$ \text{ xx}}{\text{1 Day}}$$

The higher the number of clicks, the more money your ad will generate for Google. When the number of clicks increase, so will your status in the AdWords column.

NOTHING TO LOSE ON THE CONTENT NETWORK BUT CUSTOMERS

TIP: Your CTR on Google's Content Network does not affect your account's performance and since this is the case, you lose nothing but potential business by not advertising on the Content Network. A low CTR on Google's Content Network will have no bearing on how you rank within Google search pages.

In limited circumstances you may be competing with ads placed by Google for its *own* products. Does Google always reserve for itself the top spot? In the test we conducted the answer is NO. A Google advertisement for AdWords was ranked second. Google's ads appear to be under the same rules as all other ads. They must have the highest CTRs to rank first.

Google gives top placement on the search results page by multiplying each advertiser's CTR and CPC. The highest dollar amount wins (i.e., the ads that are making Google the most money). The amount of users clicking on your ad is more vital to your AdWords placement or rank than the amount you pay to Google per click. In sum, Google wants popular ads and it will reward accordingly. If you have a CPC of $50 but you only get one click-through per week, an ad with a CPC of $1 getting 51 click-throughs will rank above you. A competitor that is only paying $1 each time a user visits its Website will be placed higher in the Google ranking system than a company paying $50 for each click! Therefore, the greater the number of clicks on your ads the less you have to pay for new business and the higher you will rank in the AdWords column.

> Getting sales or opt-ins to your newsletter, etc is a two-step process. Having a high CTR on Google is only the first step. Once customers have reached your Website you must complete the sale. This cannot be stressed enough. If you have the world's best marketing campaign, but a terrible Website, you will not gain sales or opt-ins.

B. Why Physical Advertising Space is Important

The number of Google ads visible in the AdWords column without scrolling is only 6 with an Internet Explorer browser on "full screen" view. Google displays a maximum of 8 in the AdWords column, but users must scroll down to the see the last two. If the user has their browser in the "normal" view setting, the number of ads shown in the AdWords column is reduced to only 4 without scrolling! It gets even worse for content sites such as Internet news sites that may display only 2 advertisements per page! Therefore it's imperative that you rank at least in the top 4 spots on Google and content sites so that searchers are guaranteed to see your ad. If not, searchers may have to scroll down, which reduces the likelihood that your ad will be noticed.

C. The Amazing Flexibility of Google

The beauty of Google's AdWords and Image Ads is that your advertising campaign can be changed at any time for free. Try to do that with a traditional marketer. Traditional advertising is, for the most part, an unstoppable and unchangeable advertising juggernaut. Your marketing ad on a radio station will run for a set period such as 30 days. On Google you can change your ad every day or every hour if you are not getting the results you desire. You can also pause your ad at any time. Imagine being able to do this with a billboard that potentially reaches 2000 people and businesses every second.

D. The Google Discounter Works 24/7/365

Google wants your advertising campaign to succeed. It uses a kind of digital natural selection process to keep the most popular ads on top. If the amount you are paying for each click is too high, Google will automatically reduce it. That's right, Google will automatically *decrease* the amount you are paying for each click if you have a popular ad. You'll be hard pressed to find a traditional marketing outlet that will do that for you.

> Here's an example of Google's digital selection at work. Your maximum CPC is 31¢ to stay in the top spot and the second place ad drops the maximum amount it is willing to pay for each click from 30¢ to 25¢. Google will automatically drop your CPC to 26¢, but you will maintain the top spot on the search results page as long as you continue to get more clicks than your competitor.

Google's Discounter automatically reduces your CPC to the lowest cost required for your ad to stay in its position on the search results page. In the marketing world this enables you to maximize your Return-on-Investment (ROI) by targeting only customers interested in your designated keywords. Given the number of searches conducted on Google every day, the breadth of its partner sites, AdSense and the minimal costs, can your business afford not to use AdWords and Image Ads?

YOUR ROI WILL CHANGE DAILY

TIP: Be mindful that if you advertise in foreign markets on Google your ROI will fluctuate daily based upon your home currency valuation. If you are based in Canada, but sell mostly to European customers, your ROI will change based on the strength of the Canadian dollar.

E. How the Time of Day Affects Your CPC

Once advertisers' daily budgets are exhausted, their ads will stop running. What this means for you is that you will be paying different amounts for clicks on your ad during the day. Let's say you have a competitor in your ad space with whom you are constantly battling for the top spot. When your competitor's daily budget is used up, your ad will automatically be bumped to the top spot and you will be paying less per click.

BEGIN SEASONAL ADS EARLY

TIP: Under a Shop.org poll, only 22% of sellers begin their holiday marketing by mid-October, yet over 50% of holiday shoppers have already begun to shop. Beat your competition to the holiday marketplace by starting your holiday ads in early October!

F. Setting the Frequency Your Ad Will Show

Google will automatically space the number of times your ad runs if your daily budget is below the actual amount your ad could be shown. For instance, if Google recommends a daily budget of $10 per day and you only input $5 a day, your ad will run half the time. Google tries to estimate the number of impressions for your ad based upon your daily budget and the estimated number of times your keywords will be searched on in a given day. Don't be surprised if you run a search on your keyword one minute and your ad shows up, and then right after you search again and no impression is shown.

Google displays your ad evenly throughout the day so that your daily budget is not used up in the morning. This allows you to target customers who search at different hours of the day. Say your maximum CPC is $.50 and you have a daily budget set at $12. If Google forecasts that you will receive 24 clicks a day, then when your ad initially begins, Google may display an impression once every hour. If the day is nearing its end and your ad has only received enough clicks to use up $6 of your $12, Google will begin showing more impressions. It's to Google's advantage and your advantage (if you have targeted the right market) to use up your daily budget in clicks. The way Google displays your ad is a steady, evenly paced marathon in the beginning of the day, and it becomes a race later in the day.

SET DAILY BUDGET HIGH AT FIRST

TIP: When you first begin your Google marketing campaign set your daily budget very high for a day or even a week to capture all the potential clicks you could be receiving. Once you determine that amount, you can optimize your daily budget accordingly.

III. Ad Stylization and Image Ads

A. Ad Title/Body/URL Lines Overview

Below is a representative AdWords promotion as it would appear in the right-hand column next to the Google search results. Following it is a demonstration on dos and don'ts for each line and optimization techniques.

Title Line:	Overture & Yahoo Advertising	Grab Attention Immediately
Bodyline1:	Plus 110 Tips & Tricks.	Make Bodylines Flow in
Bodyline2:	Read the Definitive Guide.	Sentence Form
URL Line:	BottleTreeBooks.com	Make URL Easy to Remember
Region:	New York	States/Metropolitan/City Region

1. Title Line

The Title of your ad must grab attention immediately and distill your advertising message. There is no time to waste given the many ads that may be competing for precious user clicks. Google allows 25 characters on the Title Line, including spaces, so make each count. This is the only section of your ad that users click on to get to your Website.

PLACE KEYWORDS IN YOUR TITLE

TIP: The highest performing ads have keywords in the Title Line, which means they will be bolded when an impression is shown. This is one of the most important factors in getting your ad click on.

Let's consider a Title for the keyword "Silk." Note how the keyword is bolded by Google, which makes the ad standout in the AdWords column.

Good Title: Silk imports

Better Title: Got Silk? Silk imports

We have used the keyword twice in the Title, which creates two bolded words in the Title alone! Customers view ads with bolded keywords as being of high quality.

CAPITALIZE WORDS IN YOUR TITLE

TIP: Capitalize Title Line words to make your ad stand apart.

Even Better Title: Got Silk? Silk Imports

MAKE THE KEYWORD FIRST IN YOUR TITLE

TIP: Some of the highest CTRs result from having the keyword first in the Title Line. Since users read from left to right, make the keyword the first word in your Title.

Superior Title: Silk Imports-Got Silk?

2. Bodylines

The two AdWords lines that form the body of the text are the substance of your advertisement. Here is where you define why your product or services are the best. You have 70 total characters in which to accomplish this (35 per line). The Title and Bodylines should flow.

DO NOT MAKE TITLE AND BODYLINES ONE SENTENCE

TIP: It's not recommended to make the Title Line and Bodylines one long sentence because of the way AdWords impressions are shown within the Google Search Network. For instance, AOL places the Title Line and Bodylines on one line, separated by a semicolon. If you make your Title and Bodylines one long sentence, you will have a semicolon appearing in the middle of them on AOL.

Make the Bodylines one long sentence or separate the Bodylines with punctuation. Many companies in the Search Network put the title and URL lines on the same line, separated by a hyphen, Bodylines underneath.

This enables search engines to maximize the number of Google advertisements that fit on a searcher's screen.

ORDER OF THE BODYLINES IS IMPORTANT

TIP: You can increase your CTR substantially by merely switching the order in which your Bodylines are placed within the ad. Get your key marketing phrase beneath the Title Line. Remember, Internet users scan even quicker than someone looking at a newspaper so getting your attention grabbing ideas pushed to the top left of the ad will increase your clicks.

Spread out your keywords within the ad to draw greater attention. If you are able to get the keyword placed within the Title and only one Bodyline, have the Bodyline keyword pushed to the right side of the ad so that it is not under the keyword that starts off the Title. If the keyword appears in the Title and *both* Bodylines, form a > type arrangement of keywords within the ad. This is best seen in the examples below:

Silk Imports
10-30% Off **Silk**.
Free Shipping Every Order.
[Website].com

Here the highlighted keywords take on a backslash (\) look through the ad to gain attention on each side of the ad. This is good keyword balancing.

Silk Imports
10-30% Off **Silk**.
Silk-Finest Quality!
[Website].com

With the keyword bolded on each line and Silk in the first Bodyline offset to the right, the forward arrow (>) formation enhances the keyword focus of the ad instead of the 3 keywords being stacked one on top of the other as the first word in each of the first 3 lines.

<u>Silk</u> Imports-Got **Silk**?
30% Off **Silk**-Free Shipping.
Silk Cheap at **Silk** Imports.
[Website].com

> This ad may seem like keyword overkill, but if you can get your marketing message across and still use numerous keyword placements within the ad, all the better. Notice the (X) spacing of the keywords.

3. URL Line

Similar to the Bodylines, the URL line is limited to 35 characters. It must include the domain extension, for example: .com, .net, .org, or .biz. The linking address, which may be different than your URL Line, must link to an active Website. You must pause any ad linking to a site that is under construction or down for maintenance. In addition, you cannot link to an email address or a file (e.g., an image, audio, video, or document file that requires an additional program or application to open or run it).

DISPLAY A DOMAIN NAME WITH RELEVANCE

TIP: If offering computer consulting services, a high-tech sounding domain name will get more clicks on an identical ad than a low-tech name.

It's interesting to note that Google does not allow you to click on the URL line, only the Title. The key for this line is to get people to remember your URL even after they have left AdWords and also to have a domain name that indicates your specialty in the products or services you're offering. Note that even if a keyword is part of your URL, that part of the URL will not be bolded by Google.

KEEP DOMAIN NAME AS SHORT AS POSSIBLE

TIP: If people can simply type in BottleTreeBooks.com to visit your Website, do not put www.BottleTreeBooks.com on the URL line, or worse yet http://www.BottleTreeBooks.com The hypertext protocol and World Wide Web letters only serve as a barrier to people remembering your Website address!

Google does not allow pop-up ads on the linking page. How does Google define "pop-ups"? Any window, regardless of content, that is opened in addition to the regular window upon entering or leaving the linked page. The back button must also be enabled at your linking Website so that users can easily return to the Google search page or ad network page. Finally, your site should use a secure server (https://) when collecting personal information from Google users.

4. Region Line

As will be discussed in greater detail below, Google allows you to specify the region in which your ad will run when searched on by people in that region. If you run a Google Local ad, Google will display the city or metropolitan region on the last line of the ad. You will have no control over this line, but its inclusion by Google makes your ad stand apart from the others because it has 5 lines instead of the 4 traditional lines.

B. Definitive Ad Stylization

The way in which AdWords are stylized is key to making your ad stand apart. If you pick wrongly, your ad will seem like a blur of words and characters that will blend in with all the other ads. If you select your words and stylization correctly, your ad will convey more of your marketing message and stand apart from the rest of the ads. Highly optimized ads will get you the most clicks even if you do not have top placement within the AdWords column.

USE GRAMMAR & SPELL CHECK

TIP: Cut and paste spell-checked and grammar-checked verbiage into a new ad. For the vast majority of Internet customers your Google advertisement will be their first introduction to your products and services. A spelling mistake in a small Internet ad is the equivalent of having a large, misspelled business sign outside your office.

1. Style/Interior Punctuation

Fonts: The AdWords default font is Times New Roman, regular, 10 point. This cannot be changed.

Capitals: Capitals can be used in AdWords. The first letter of *each* word is permitted to be a capital and is a great way to make your ad stand out from all the others.

Stylization: Bold/Italics/Underlines/Small Caps/Bullets cannot be copied into AdWords from a word processing program such as Microsoft Word.

Commas: Avoid the serial comma. It uses a precious character.

Good	Bad
Boats and Motor Homes Eight Brands, Makes and Models. Ship Anywhere-Fast. [Website].com	Boats and Motor Homes Eight brands, makes, and models. Ship anywhere – fast. http:\\www.[Website].com
Why?	**Why?**
<ul><li>Capitalization of each word.</li><li>No use of serial comma (1 char. saved).</li><li>Essential part of domain name used (11 char. saved).</li></ul>	<ul><li>No capitalization of each word.</li><li>Use of the serial comma.</li><li>URL Line has unnecessary characters (http: \\www.). Domain name is hard to read and extra characters make it less likely to be remembered.</li></ul>

2. Style/Interior Punctuation Continued

Apostrophes: Avoid use with decades or acronyms.

Semicolons: Semicolons may be used. Note that a semicolon uses two characters versus a hyphen not surrounded by spaces.

Hyphens: Do not use spaces surrounding your hyphen. It wastes two precious characters you might need later.

Slashes: Slashes are not allowed outside of the URL Line.

Spaces: Spaces must be used in normal context on the Title Line. Use only one space after a period instead of two.

Good	Bad
Boats and Motor Homes Eight Brands & Makes. Ship Anywhere-Fast. 90s Models. [Website].com	Boats - Motor Homes Eight brands/makes. Ship anywhere – fast. 90's Models. [Website].com
Why?	**Why?**
• No spaces around hyphen (2 char. saved). • No slash. • No apostrophe in decade.	• Improper use of spaces in title. • Slash used improperly. • Spaces surrounding the hyphen. • Apostrophe used in decade.

3. Abbreviations/Shorthand/Symbols

Shorthand and symbols (found under the Insert dropdown in Word and WordPerfect) can be used in your ad, but they must be used in the proper context.

+: Use as addition symbol, or instead of "plus."

Lb: Exchange for weight "pound."

£:   Exchange for monetary "pound."

Nos or #:   Truncate "numbers."

Large Numbers: Use "100s" instead of "hundreds;" "1000s" instead of "thousands."

TV: Instead of "television."

CD: Instead of "Compact Disc" or "CD-ROM."

Countries/States: Use country abbreviations like UK instead of "United Kingdom." Use providence or state abbreviations such as TN instead of "Tennessee."

$:   Only use to denote dollars (e.g., $10.99), do not use to replace "money" or "price."

PLACE SYMBOLS IN YOUR TEXT AD TO GET ATTENTION

TIP: The trick to getting symbols placed in your ad is to copy and paste them from a word processing document. Some of Google's syndication partners may not display them, however, so keep this in mind.

Good	Bad
Workout Depot #1 Brands + Size Clothes-All Dumbbell Lbs. Low Prices. As Seen on TV. [Website].com	Workout Depot--Best Brands Plus size clothing. As seen on TV. All Dumbbell Pounds. Low $. http:\\www.[Website].com
Why?	**Why?**
• # used for "number" (5 char. saved). • + instead of "Plus" (3 char. saved). • Lbs replaced "pounds" (3 char. saved). • Prices spelled out. • TV used for "television" (10 char. saved).	• Best used instead of the shorter "#1," which also draws more attention. • Spelled out "pounds." • $ is improper in this context. • Television spelled out.

4. Abbreviations/Shorthand/Symbols Continued

%:   Insert for "percentage."

@:   Replaces "at."

?:   Use instead of "question."

&:   Never waste characters by spelling out "and." Use the ampersand instead.

0-10:   Use instead of spelling out the number.

Special typographical fonts will not be displayed in AdWords. Fonts such as Webdings and Wingdings cannot be displayed in your Google ad. Cutting and pasting these symbols will result in the underlying character being placed in the ad instead of the symbol.

Good	Bad
Boats & Motor Homes 8 Brands: 20% Off. High Quality @ Low Prices. [Website].com	Boats and Motor Homes Eight Brands-Twenty Percent Off. High Quality at Low Prices. [Website].com
Why?	**Why?**
<ul><li>& exchanged for "and" (2 char. saved).</li><li>8 substituted for "eight" (4 char. saved).</li><li>20 replaced "Twenty" (4 char. saved).</li><li>% used for "Percent" (7 char. saved).</li><li>@ used for "at" (1 char. saved).</li></ul>	<ul><li>Used "and."</li><li>Spelled out "Eight."</li><li>Used "Twenty."</li><li>Spelled out "Percent."</li><li>At used instead of "@."</li></ul>

PLACE LOCAL REGION NAME IN TEXT AD

TIP: If you offer a local service or product, include the name in the ad. Potential local customers in Memphis are much more likely to click on an ad with "Memphis" than a generic, national sounding ad.

Good	Bad
Memphis Stereos for Less Free CD w/Purchase! Never a ? of Trust. [Website].com	Stereos 4 Less Free CD with Purchase! See Our Gr8 Prices! [Website].com
Why?	**Why?**
<ul><li>Memphis region defined.</li><li>CD substituted for "compact disk" (10 char. saved).</li><li>W/ replaces "with" (2 char. saved).</li><li>? used instead of "Question" (7 char. saved).</li></ul>	<ul><li>No mention of local region.</li><li>4 not used in number context and is not allowed.</li><li>Excessive use of shorthand makes ad unprofessional.</li><li>"gr8" is not used in normal context. "License plate" lingo is not allowed.</li></ul>

5. Legal Terminology

Registered Trademarks: ® denotes a registered trademark or service mark.

Non-Registered Trademarks: tm denotes a trademark that has not been registered.

Non-Registered Service Marks: (sm) denotes a service mark that has not been registered.

Copyrights: © replaces copyright.

SEARCH TRADEMARKS FOR FREE

TIP: You can search registered trademarks for free at the U.S. Patent & Trademark Office: www.USPTO.gov. Canadian http://strategis.ic.gc.ca/sc_mrksv/cipo/welcome//welcome.html offers trademark searches. Here is Australia's Trademark Office Website www.ipaustralia.gov.au for searching. In Europe, you can search Community Trademarks for free at the European Union http://oami.eu.int/en/default.htm. In Asia, you can search trademarks in China at www.ChinaTrademarkOffice.com. India also has a searchable trademark database: http://www.ipindia.nic.in/.

Familiarize yourself with Google's policy for using trademarks in your ad or keywords. At present, Google will investigate complaints from trademark owners only related to trademarks used within AdWords text and it will suspend the ad in its discretion. If suspended, an advertiser must submit a new ad with the trademark term deleted. Google is trying to prevent confusion in the marketplace, a hallmark of trademark infringement. For instance, if the trademark Coke is used in an ad, but the company only sells Pepsi products, then searchers may be confused in clicking on the ad in the mistaken belief they will find Coke products for sale.

Google does not limit the use of trademarks as keywords. This does not mean, however, that competitors will agree with their trademarked keywords being used to drive traffic to another Website.

Note that Google's Trademark Complaint Procedure www.google.com/tm_complaint.html varies for trademarks rights in the U.S. and Canada, versus trademark rights elsewhere.

SEARCH YELLOW PAGES & WHITE PAGES AROUND THE WORLD

TIP: There may be instances when you need to check if a business exists in a local market before starting your Google marketing campaign. www.AnyWho.com offers free yellow and white page searches for over 30 countries.

Good	Bad
"Coffee w/Poe"-Amazon.com® Historical Novel of Poe's Life, Loves & Letters! © Andrew Barger. [Website].com	"Coffee w/Poe"-Amazon.com Historical Novel of Poe's Life. Copyright-Andrew Barger. [Website].com
Why?	**Why?**
<ul><li>® denotes registered trademark.</li><li>Bodylines flow together.</li><li>© replaces Copyright (8 char. saved).</li></ul>	<ul><li>No trademark designations noted.</li><li>Copyright is spelled out.</li></ul>

6. Punctuation & Contractions

Periods: Use at the end of first and second Bodylines to make them read like sentences. Alternatively, one long sentence can span the first and second Bodylines. Also, use only one space after a period in your ad instead of the traditional two spaces.

Exclamations: The Title Line cannot have an exclamation point and the Bodylines may only have one exclamation point.

Question Marks: No limits as long as they are used appropriately.

Repetition: Repetition of punctuation or words is not allowed.

Contractions: Use these negative-sounding words sparingly.

Good	Bad
Boats & Motor Homes 20 Brands: 20% Off! Why Go Anywhere Else? [Website].com	Boats & Motor Homes! 20 Brands-20% Off Low, Low, Low $-Intrigued?? [Website].com
Why?	**Why?**
• No exclamation in Title Line. • Exclamation used at end of 1st Bodyline. • No unnecessary repetition. • Single Question mark is proper.	• Exclamation point not allowed in Title Line. • No use of period at end of 1st Bodyline so it will not read like a sentence when combined with the 2nd Bodyline. • Invalid repetition of "Low." • Double question marks are not allowed.

USE TELEPHONE NUMBERS IN YOUR AD

TIP: Use of numbers in your ad is a great way to save precious characters *and* to make your ad stand apart. If your business has an 800 number, use it in your AdWords campaign! The string of numbers will make your ad stand out and provide another means for customers to contact you who may have security concerns about giving information via the Internet. If advertising on Google Local, a regional telephone number may be the best way for customers to reach you and the local area code will identify you with that region.

If only minor changes are required (e.g., removing a question mark or correcting a spelling mistake) for an ad to comply with Google's Editorial Guidelines, an AdWords Specialist may edit your ad. Google will not, however, take responsibility for fixing all ads. Please ensure your advertisement meets the Editorial Guidelines prior to running the ad so that it does not get suspended.

7. Call-to-Action & Generic Words

"Click Now": Improper Call-to-Action.

"Click Here": Improper Call-to-Action.

"Click on Me": Improper Call-to-Action.

"Look Here": Improper Call-to-Action.

"Visit Here": Improper Call-to-Action.

"Look at This": Improper Call-to-Action.

"This Site is": Improper generic phrase.

The second Bodyline cannot extend into the URL line.

Good	Bad
Boats & Motor Homes 20 Brands: 20% Off! Visit the Motor Home Specialist. [Website].com	Boats & Motor Homes! 20 Brands-20% Off Look at Me to See what you Need. [Website].com
Why?	**Why?**
• Proper call to action based on unique business model.	• Improper call-to-action. • Bodyline 2 bleeds into the URL line.

No inappropriate language is allowed, including swearing or that deemed offensive (i.e., politically incorrect). Be careful of what region your ads are targeted as some words may be offensive there. "Bloody" is a curse word in the UK but not in the US.

Three Categories of Ads

Ads are placed into 3 special categories by Google's editors:

1. Family Safe
2. Non-Family Safe
3. Adult Sexual Content

Google allows all three types of ads, but its partners on the Google Network may not.

Google will not deliver anything other than "Family-Safe" ads through the Content Network or Gmail no matter what the article or email message is about.

C. Image Ads

In 2004 Google announced the availability of Image Ads for its AdSense customers. This came as a surprise to many in the Internet advertising world given Google's previous distaste for graphic advertising. The ads can be uploaded to Google in the following formats:

- .JPG
- .GIF
- .PNG

Only "family safe" images are allowed on Image Ads and they cannot blink or move in any fashion.

Google does not show Image Ads on its Website. They are only shown on Websites enabled with AdSense advertising.

1. Sizes

Of the 11 square and rectangle sizes in which AdSense ads are displayed, Image Ads may only be created in four of the rectangular sizes:

Image Ad Formats

- Leaderboard [Shape: Horizontal Rectangle] (728x90)
- Banner [Shape: Horizontal Rectangle] (468x60)
- Skyscraper [Shape: Vertical Rectangle] (120x600)
- Medium Rectangle [Shape: Vertical Rectangle] (300x250)

Visit www.google.com/adsense/adformats to see samples of each size.

Image ads, given their size, displace a number of AdWords textual advertisements on each AdSense site. Therefore, the major downside to running an Image Ad campaign is that your ad must receive 2 to 4 times as many clicks as a text ad. This means at 10 to 20 clicks per 1000 impressions. Since Image Ads usually displace 2 to 4 text ads, Google requires a higher CTR for image ads.

2. Image Ad Advertising Space

Creating an Image Ad on Google has its advantages. The advantages are that the ad grabs the attention of users quicker than text ads. We know that if Google shows your ad on an AdSense Website it will displace a number of test ads. What a great way to drive out your competition!

RUN BOTH IMAGE ADS AND ADWORDS

TIP: Run both Image Ads and text ads for your marketing campaign so your advertising is assured broad coverage. Google does not allow AdSense Websites to display only Image Ads on a page. They have the option to either have text only ads or a combination of text and graphical ads on a page. This allows Google to channel only the most relevant, click-worthy ads to your Website.

> Google requires that your Image Ad have relevance to your keywords. If you have selected rakes, shovels, and hoes as your keywords, you must show garden tools in your image ad.

3. Colors

The colors you pick for your Image Ads are vitally important to their success. They are no less significant than text for AdWords. Remember also, that limited text can be used in your Image Ads. Strive to adopt the same attention-getting principles used throughout this book for Image Ad text. Following are tips for getting your Image Ad noticed and for avoiding confusing tone combinations.

a. Foreground vs. Background Contrasts

Using a light background color with dark text is the preferred method of viewing Image Ads on the Internet. This way the text jumps off the page at searchers. This is the same technique Web designers have used since the mid-nineties.

BE CAREFUL OF BORDER COLORS

TIP: Ensure the tones of your ad work well in multiple border colors. AdSense Websites can change the border colors of Image Ads.

If you do not use text in your Image Ad, make key images dark with a pale background color.

AVOID CLOSELY-RELATED COLORS

TIP: Tones that are closely related such as yellows and greens, and reds and greens are called "vibrating" colors. The human eye sometimes has difficulty distinguishing between the two. This is especially the case for "color blind" Internet users. Avoid use of these vibrating colors to ensure all parts of your ad can be seen clearly.

Google will add a "Feedback - Ad by Google" link near the bottom or corner of your Image Ad for the Leaderboard, Banner, and Medium Rectangle sizes. The "Feedback - Ad by Google" link will be placed at the bottom of Skyscraper ads.

b. Apply the Four Color Rule

What is often mistakenly called the "Three Color Rule" is actually a guideline for applying Web colors that should be followed with Image Ads. Specifically, the rule states that one background color (preferably pale) should be used in conjunction with only three foreground colors, hence the "Four Color Rule." A blend of additional foreground colors makes the ad too busy and more than a subtle use of multiple background colors will hamper reading of the foreground colors.

> The 3-color foreground rule of thumb applies to any text that you may incorporate into your Image Ad. The colored text, even if it is black or white, will use up 1 of your targeted 3 colors.

c. The Universal Browser Color Palette

Various Web browsers may display some colors differently than intended. This can wreck havoc with an Image Ad. To be safe, use one of the 216 browser-safe colors. They will look the same on every browser for every color monitor. Although there is not enough space to display them here, conduct an Internet search on the "216 browser-safe colors" to show them along with background information on using them.

IV.   Keyword Creation and Management

A. Keywords Are Key

Google rewards relevance and relevance only comes by fine-tuning your ads to appear when keywords (i.e., search terms) are used linking your products or services to potential customer interests. Not only are keywords of primary importance, but also the type of ad. You can choose the most relevant keywords in the world, but if your ad is not compelling, potential customers will not click on it.

LET GOOGLE CRAFT YOUR MARKETING CAMPAIGN

TIP: Deciding which keywords are best for your online marketing campaign can be daunting. Realizing this, Google allows new subscribers to have its AdWords Specialists craft your ad and choose the best keywords for only $299 USD.

There are two ways you can approach your initial marketing campaign on Google: Use a few, highly targeted keywords or use a large number of keywords, selecting both specific and broad keywords to later funnel your keywords to the ones resulting in the most purchases. The approach you select depends on your target market. We'll discuss each in detail below.

1. The Highly Targeted Keywords Campaign

When a Google advertising campaign is first started it is normal to choose broad or generic search terms so that an advertisement is displayed numerous times. This catchall tactic is absolutely the wrong one to take if you are marketing specific products. If you have a defined market and specific products or services for that market, start your campaign with a few highly targeted keywords. If you are selling a rare Delorian sports car, target the keywords "Delorian," "Delorean," "Delorian sports car," and "Delorean sports car," etc. There is no need to apply a dragnet approach to advertising this very specific product that is targeted at an equally specific market.

If, for example, you are marketing soccer gear, the generic keyword "soccer" would be too broad. Under this scenario your ads would appear when people searched on the terms "soccer moms" "soccer stadiums," "rules of soccer," etc. Your ads would be appearing for terms not associated with your business and that are unlikely to increase business. The ads would rank low in the AdWords column because they would have a low CTR. And, even if users did click on your ad, they would be unlikely to buy your products, which means you would be wasting ad dollars in the form of low ROI.

DESIGNATE A SEPARATE CPC FOR EACH KEYWORD

TIP: Google's Power Posting Tool allows you to set a unique CPC for *each* keyword. If you have a highly targeted ad campaign, designate a separate CPC for each keyword. If your average position is shown to be low on the Traffic Estimator Tool, increase the amount per click you are willing to pay for that keyword. If you already have the #1 position when only paying $.05 per click, there is no reason to pay Google more. You would be throwing money away. In addition, be aware that Google always rounds up your bid amount to the nearest hundredth place. For instance, a $.075 USD per click bid will be rounded up to $.08 USD.

When you are editing your keywords you can designate different hyperlinks for different keywords even though the identical ad impression will be shown. For example, if your Website specializes in music by the Beatles, most keywords would link to your home page of Beatles CDs. If, however, a person types in the keywords "John Lennon," you can link it to your John Lennon CD page within your Website. Google makes a seemingly difficult task easy.

Use Specific Keywords and Phrases

When you set up your AdWords or Image Ads campaign Google will display the average number of searches users conduct on that term every day. There is no need for a shotgun approach to advertising with Google. Your exact target market is defined! Consider the online soccer product store. Instead of using the broad keyword "soccer," use

the following specific keywords:
- Soccer Balls
- Shin Guards
- Soccer Shorts

You can then further narrow the times when your ad is triggered for these keywords by using Exact Match or Phrase Match, which is discussed below.

If you can find keywords that your competitors have missed, or that have few others bidding on them, you will have much less competition when impressions of your ad are shown on Google. How can you learn which keywords your competitors are bidding on? It's simple. Use Google's Traffic Estimator Tool that is located under the Tools bar within the Campaign Management tab. Here's an example that was conducted on the following keywords:

Keywords	Clicks/Day	Avg. CPC	Cost/Day	Avg. Position
Antique Flower Vases	< 0.1	$0.05	$0.00	30.3
Antique Vases	7.1	$0.05	$0.36	6.9
Old Flower Vases	< 0.1	$0.05	$0.00	1.0
Antique Vases	< 0.1	$0.05	$0.00	2.4

This simple chart tells us volumes about a potential marketing campaign for antique flower vases.

a. Clicks/Day
Under this column the keywords "Antique Vases" will garner over 7 forecasted clicks per day while the others will result in less than .1 clicks. Right away we see that this is where the most searches are conducted. But if you specialize in antique flower vases, this may result in clicks and ad money spent on people searching for vases that are neither antique nor suited for flowers.

b. Avg. CPC

Here we have set the Cost-Per-Click to the lowest amount allowed by Google.

c. Cost/Day

We see that the keywords "Antique Vases" will gain the most clicks and result in $0.36 being spent per day.

d. Avg. Position

This column ranks the average position in which your ad impression will be placed in the AdWords column. Note that the keywords resulting in the most clicks will not necessarily result in the lowest placement. "Antique Flower Vases" has less than .01 forecasted clicks per day yet the average position is a low 30.3 at $.05 per click. What does this tell us? Competitors are paying large sums per click for the keywords "Antique Flower Vases" when the most traffic is under "Antique Vases." Look for similar opportunities in your market area.

2. The Keyword Funneling Campaign

If your products or services cater to a large number of potential customers, pick at least 50 keywords and then cull them down to the top 10 or 15 that are getting you the most sales. The mistake many advertisers make is trying to pin down the top 10 keywords from the start, which is difficult at best until a click-through track record has been established. For instance, if you sell many types of hammers, you may list the normal keywords such as "claw hammers," "sledge hammers," "ball ping hammers," etc. But a better initial keyword campaign would be to include those keywords plus others such as "rubber hammers," "metal hammers," "discount hammers," "mallets," "hammer enthusiasts," "hammer collectors," "Stanley hammers," "Black & Decker hammers," etc. You may learn that the Internet is full of users searching under "mallets" instead of "rubber hammers."

The downside to broad keywords, as will be discussed in greater detail below, is that they may lead to mis-clicks. For instance, if your business is antiquities and you're offering President Abraham Lincoln memorabilia, the broad keyword "Lincoln" may attract mis-clicks by those interested in Lincoln automobiles or Lincoln, Nebraska. Avoid unwanted clicks by people who are unlikely to buy your product or services. The ultimate goal with Google advertising is not to increase visits to your Website but rather to increase sales.

3. Similar Keywords

In addition to focusing your broad search term on more specific terms, Google also provides a selection of similar keywords within the results of its Keyword Suggestion Tool. These will not contain your broad search term, but will offer search terms that are close. Note that most of the similar terms will be relevant, but some are clearly not within a particular industry and you can cull these immediately. Conducting a broad search on "hammers" under Google's Keyword Suggestion Tool resulted in the suggestion of 4 "more specific keywords" and over 100 "similar keywords."

4. Keyword Matching Options

Change keyword matching options to better target your ads. By specifying the types of keyword matching options that will trigger your ads, you can widen or narrow your focus to prospective customers.

Five Keyword Matching Options
a. Broad b. Expanded c. Phrase d. Exact e. Negative

Keyword matching does not apply to AdWords and Image Ads selected to show in Google's Content Network.

a. Broad Match

Broad Match is the biggest net you have as an advertiser to gain customers. In most instances, however, it is too big and not recommended. With this net you will likely catch Internet users that are not interested in your products or services, which is simply a waste of your advertising money. You want to catch the big fish and let the little ones swim through your net. Here's an example: Say your Broad Match keywords are "Football Shoes." This means that impressions of your ad will show for the keyword "Football" or "Shoes" even if other words are included in the search. Under this example impressions of the ad would show for "Ballerina Shoes," "Bowling Shoes," and "Shoes Worn by Elvis." Needless to say, your ad would have a low CTR for these Broad Match terms.

Under Broad Matching, ad impressions appear for queries that don't exactly match keywords. This means there is an increased chance your ad will not be relevant and thereby a higher chance it will be disabled. The keyword variations and expanded Broad Matching are monitored closely and can be disabled by Google if they don't achieve a high enough relevance factor.

b. Expanded Match

If you select Broad Matching, your keywords will automatically be included in Expanded Matching. This means Google's computer algorithms will show impressions of your ad for keywords that closely match your selected keywords or that are slight variations. Expanded Matching includes synonyms, related phrases, and plurals, even if they aren't in your keyword lists. Expanded matching allows your ad to show more often and be linked to search terms that are relevant to your marketing campaign. Under Expanded Match the keywords "stop sign" may result in impressions of your ad showing when "traffic light" is searched on.

HOW TO STOP EXPANDED MATCHING

TIP: Expanded Match terms can be stopped by adding them as Negative keywords. You can also change Broad Match keywords to Exact or Phrase Match keywords to eliminate Expanded Matching.

Google will automatically change Expanded Matches over time based upon which keywords best fit the intent of your ad. This artificial intelligence feature shows your ad for only the alternate keywords and phrases that are getting you the most clicks. It also learns additional keywords and phrases to show your ad when searched upon. Remember, the more clicks your ad gets, the more money Google makes. Google wants your ad to succeed!

FIND ADDITIONAL KEYWORDS

TIP: The Keyword Suggestion Tool displays additional keywords that could trigger impressions of your ad. Once again there is no charge for this powerful tool Google provides. More below.

c. Phrase Match

Phrase Match requires that the exact keywords, in the exact order must be included in the search for an ad impression to show. Other words may also be included. For instance, let's consider our "Football Shoes" example. Under this scenario the search term "Leather Football Shoes" would trigger an impression, but "Shoes for Football" would not.

Expanded Matching is not available for Phrase Match.

d. Exact Match

Exact Match means just what it says. The *exact* keywords must be used in the search and the keywords must be in the *exact* order. No other words can be included. If the Exact Match Keywords are "Football Shoes," then "Red Football Shoes" will not invoke an impression of your ad and neither will "Football Shoe."

e. Negative Match

Negative keywords are a great way to prevent wasted clicks that drain your advertising budget. You can use Negative Match in addition to one of the other 4 keyword matching options. You can use Google's Negative Keyword Tool to select negative keywords or simply place a minus sign in front of a word. If your negative keyword is "white," anyone searching on "White Football Shoes" will not see an impression of your ad.

There are certain instances where you want to use negative keywords to ensure that your ads do not appear even when your company is discussed online. For instance, if you do not want a product ad running next to negative earnings results about your company, you can use negative keywords such as "–revenue."

USE NEGATIVE KEYWORDS

TIP: If there has been negative media press relating to your industry as a whole, you may not want your ads showing for certain negative keywords such as investigation, etc.

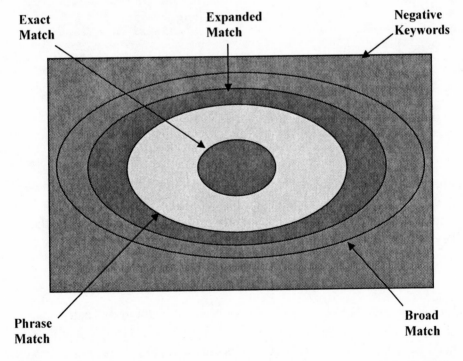

Exact Match

Expanded Match

Negative Keywords

Phrase Match

Broad Match

Consider the following chart using the "Football Shoes" example for bid upon keywords. The chart shows when an impression of the ad would be shown on the following search terms.

Search Term	Broad Match	Expanded Match	Phrase Match	Exact Match
Red Shoes	Yes	Yes	No	No
Green Shoes	Yes	Yes	No	No
Red Football Shoes	Yes	Yes	Yes	No
Football Shoes	Yes	Yes	Yes	Yes

5. Monitoring Your Keyword Performance

Monitoring which keywords are resulting in the most clicks is fundamental to having a highly effective marketing campaign. Google once again makes this easy by providing a status column for each keyword within an AdGroup.

Five Ad Statuses

1. Normal;
2. In Trial;
3. On Hold;
4. Disabled;
5. Suspended.

a. Normal

Previously listed as the "Strong" and "Moderate" categories, the new Normal listing keywords have a minimum CTR of 5 clicks per 1000 impressions. If your ad is consistently ranked in this category in the keyword status column, leave it alone. There is no need to mess with success.

b. In Trial

Previously labeled by Google as "At Risk," the ads in this category are close to having a CTR that has fallen below.5% for Google itself. You need your ad to be as effective as possible and Google is simply warning you that work needs to be done. Use the tips and optimizers provided in *Google Advertising A-Z* and you should be back on track in no time. In Trial ads will be shown until Google is confident that they are statistically above or below the .5% click level. Once determined, Google will: (1)

place the ad back into Normal status; (2) put the ad into Slowed status, which means it needs refining; or (3) place the ad into Hold status.

> The obvious solution may appear that you should click on your *own* ad to get its CTR up. This, however, is a losing strategy. Not only are you wasting advertising click money, you are merely putting a bandage on an injured ad that really needs stitches. This quick fix will not solve the ultimate issues with your ad. Either the ad itself is not compelling or you have targeted the wrong keywords.

Trial-Slowed status is merely a warning sign that your ad and keyword combinations are not meshing well. When this happens your ad is in the Google doghouse for those particular keywords and will begin showing less frequently. To get back to Normal status you must optimize the ad. Make targeted changes as shown in this book and see where it leads. A common cause is the use of Broad Matching, which results in more impressions but potentially less clicks. Remember that in Google the number of clicks you are getting is paramount to the success of your ad and how Google categorizes and ranks it in the advertising column.

c. On Hold
If you have keywords that are performing below the minimum CTR and the limited number of In Trial keywords have been met within your account, these underperforming keywords will be put into On Hold status. Google will disable these ads and they will stop showing. All is not lost, however. As In Trial space frees up within your account, these On Hold keywords will be automatically bumped up to In Trial status.

d. Disabled
Disabled status is the death knell for your keywords. Ads for these keywords will no longer show impressions. They reach this status in two ways. First, if you have a keyword that is performing poorly it will be shut down. Second, if you have a keyword that has not garnered a click in 90 days it will be placed in Disabled status.

DELETE DISABLED KEYWORDS IMMEDIATELY

TIP: Disabled keywords affect the impression performance of not only your AdGroup, but also your entire Campaign if used in multiple places. Monitor your AdGroups frequently and delete Disabled keywords.

Seasonal ads may be Disabled after the holidays are over due to lack of clicks within 90 days. To prevent this, pause or delete your seasonal ad immediately after the holidays and then fire it up again next year. If you forget and your seasonal ad gets Disabled, you have a few options. First, delete all your keywords for the seasonal ad. Second, create a new AdGroup with the deleted keywords when the next holiday season rolls around.

December 14th is the busiest shopping day of the year and sales taper off until January, which is the slowest month of shopping for most businesses.

e. Suspended

If Google's editors find that an ad violates one of its policies such as trademark usage, it will place the ad in Suspended status until the ad is edited to come in line with the guidelines. Suspended status will cause the ad to stop showing.

B. Abbreviations, Plurals & Misspellings

Google's advertising system is centered on performance. The ads getting the clicks are the ones that receive top placement and the ones not getting traffic will eventually stop being displayed. That's why it is essential that your ad stick out from the others. Below are tips on how to make it happen. Your ad can stop running for certain keywords no matter how much you are paying per click! It's the clicks that count most. Abbreviations, plurals and misspellings are a great way to get additional clicks on certain keywords and phrases that your competitors may not cover. Google's Keyword Tool will suggest these variations for you! Use the Keyword Tool in combination with your own industry knowledge to select keywords that your competitors are missing.

Use Abbreviations, Plurals and Misspellings

A hammer store might include the following keywords in its AdGroup for Mallets:

- ➢ Mallet *(Correct Spelling)*
- ➢ Mallets *(Plural)*
- ➢ Malletts *(Common Misspelling)*
- ➢ Rubber Mallet *(Additional Words)*
- ➢ Rubber Mallets *(Additional Words Included with Plurals or Misspellings)*

CREATE AN ADGROUP FOR EACH SET OF KEYWORDS

TIP: Instead of having one ad of which identical impressions are shown for *every* keyword, breakdown the keywords by group and have tailored ads for each.

Below are examples of AdGroups set up for a "Mallet" product line and variations of the keyword that a competitor may not consider, including a misspelling.

Keyword:	• Mallets

AdGroup 1
Mallets-Low Cost   20-25% Off Mallets.   Mallets-15 Brands!   [Website].com
• Title includes exact plural keyword, which means it will be bolded.

- Keyword used again in Bodylines, which mean it will be bolded again. Note the (>) keyword configuration within the ad.

ONE LETTER MAKES ALL THE DIFFERENCE

TIP: When a search is conducted, Google bolds words in your ad that exactly match words in the search. Lack of *one* letter can make your ad get lost in the AdWords shuffle. Google will not highlight "Mugs" on a search for "Mug." Likewise, "Mug" will not be bolded on a search for "Mugs." This AdWords shortcoming can be remedied if you slightly change your ad for various plurals that will allow key terms in your ad to be highlighted by Google.

Keyword:	• Mallet

AdGroup 2

Mallet
20-25% Mallet Savings.
15 Mallet Brands!
[Website].com

- Title matches keyword, which means it will be bolded.
- Keyword used again in Bodylines, which mean it will be bolded in three lines of the ad.

THE TRICK TO MISSPELLED KEYWORDS

TIP: In two instances customers will misspell your product name when searching. The first is the obvious typo situation where they hit the wrong key. The second is when they are unsure of how to spell the product name. This is the only time you want a typo reflected in your ad, but limit it only to the Title Line. If you set up an AdGroup for each primary misspelling of your product name and include it in only the Title, in the vast majority of instances your ad will be the *only* one with the term highlighted! Then use the correct spelling in the Bodylines just in case the potential customer is the first type of searcher and realizes they made a typo. This is a great way to advertise when your competitors may not think to do so and to make your ad stand apart with a bold misspelled keyword in the Title even if they do!

Keyword:	• Malletts

AdGroup 3

Malletts
20-50% Off Mallets.
15 Mallet Brands!
[Website].com

- Title matches misspelled keyword, which means it will be bolded.
- Keyword is spelled correctly in Bodylines, but they will not be bolded.

Keywords:	• Rubber Mallets

AdGroup 4
Rubber Mallets 10-20% Off Rubber Mallets. Rubber Mallets-15 Brands! [Website].com
• Title matches keywords, which means they will be bolded. • Keywords used again in Bodylines, which means they will be bolded.

Obviously more AdGroups can be created for the Mallet example above following this same line of logic. See what works best for your marketing campaign based off these techniques.

V.   Google Foreign Languages and Advertising Regions

A. Use Foreign Languages to Broaden Your Campaign

It is clear that geographic issues can easily arise in your Google marketing campaign given the global reach of the Internet. Fortunately, Google has made it easy to define your advertising by geographic region. You select the language(s) under which your ad will run and then select one of 5 geographic regions. Here are the 14 languages from which your ads can run in Google:

The 14 Different Keyword Languages

1. English
2. Chinese (Simplified)
3. Chinese (Traditional)
4. Danish
5. Dutch
6. Finnish
7. French
8. German
9. Italian
10. Japanese
11. Korean
12. Norwegian
13. Spanish
14. Swedish

WATCH OUT FOR KEYWORDS IN CERTAIN GEOGRAPHIC MARKETS

TIP: If you are a seller on the Internet, you may very well have an international marketplace into which you sell products or at least into different geographic regions. Be mindful of alternate terms for your products in these markets. Drinks are called "soda" in much of the southern United States, "pop" in the Midwest, and "soft drinks" in most regions around the country.

Keywords in many languages are reversed from the English version. Take, for instance, Spanish.

English user search: "Cilantro Chilies Verde"
Spanish user search: "Chilies Verde Cilantro"

USE FREE LANGUAGE TRANSLATIONS

TIP: One of the Internet's best free language translation sites is offered by Altavista. Visit http://World.Altavista.com/ to translate your keywords into the various languages of your target market.

Alternate Keywords in Other Geographic Markets

Take our soccer example for instance. In the United Kingdom, and most other countries, soccer is called "football."

More Defined Approach:
> Foot Balls
> Footballs
> Football Shorts

For the U.S. market you would simply have an AdGroup for the keyword "soccer" instead of "football."

B. Use Geographic Regions to Your Advantage

When creating your Google advertisement you will be presented with 5 geographic regions from which you may choose. How does Google know if a person is searching in a particular region? There are two ways. The first is when the searcher uses a city or state name in the search itself (e.g., Search term: "Memphis Barbeque Sauce"). Google may also compare the Internet Protocol (IP) address with a database to determine where the searcher is located. If Google cannot determine either, it will default to global/nationwide ads.

If the searcher's Internet Service Provider (ISP), uses a proxy server, Google will be unable to determine the IP address of the searcher.

Five Google Geographic Regions

1. Global
2. Nationwide
3. Regions
4. Cities
5. Customized

1. The Global Region

The global region is self-explanatory. It spans all 240 countries under the Google umbrella. If this is your target market and you are selling physical products, you must have a product that can be shipped virtually anywhere. This will likely require the consultation of a law firm dealing in international trade to ensure international trademark, copyright and patent laws will not be violated, import/export laws of various countries, etc.

REMEMBER TIME ZONE DIFFERENCES

TIP: It's easy to think no one is clicking on your ad at 3 AM, yet this may be the highest traffic time for customers in Europe. Google is tied to Pacific Standard Time, which means the Google advertising day beings at 8 GST. For European advertisers, North America will not be viewing your ads until late in the Google day.

Unlike traditional advertising, Google charges the same amount per click (from the amount you set) if you are advertising locally to a small market or globally to millions of people. If your products or services reach a global or national region, your ad will be seen more often and you will be paying the same CPC as if you were advertising to a local market of a thousand people. It's also a free way to build brand recognition in a country or internationally.

2. The National Region

The nationwide region is also self-explanatory. This region spans any of 240 countries under the Google umbrella. This will be the target market for most companies selling physical products that have a national reach such as appliances, automobile parts, books, hair care products, and others. This is an undesirable region if you are offering local services such as restaurants, house cleaning services, lawn services, etc.

3. The Amazon-Specific Marketing Campaign

Amazon.com seeks to be the Internet's largest retailer. Under its Advantage and Marketplace Programs, sellers of products can list items on Amazon.com and reach its millions of users. Now imagine coupling this reach with your Google advertising campaign. If your products are offered through Amazon, you can set up Google ads that target the six country regions in which Amazon has established stores. Apart from the United States, Amazon has international Websites targeting Austria, Canada, United Kingdom, Germany, France, and Japan. Each ad impression will have a link to a different Web page within your overall Website. For example, one of your ads may be in French and only appear to Google users in France. You URL will link to a French page within your Website that, in turn, links to www.Amazon.fr (Amazon's French Website). A more direct approach would be to link directly to www.Amazon.fr from your Google ad. To do this, however, the ad must show that you are an affiliate as discussed below.

> Ensure that the distributor for your product, ships to the country/region in which you are targeting.

4. States & Metropolitan Regions

The key to the states and metropolitan regions of Google is first determining how they are defined. Google gives you the option of choosing between entire states within a country or major metropolitan areas. For example, San Francisco-San Jose-Oakland is a metropolitan area in the State of California that you will have the option to select.

Metropolitan regions may span state borders. For example, Rochester, Minnesota-Mason City, Iowa is a region that you will have the option of selecting within Google.

All of the regions within Google's 240 countries are not available under the states and metropolitan areas option. This will be the target market for most companies selling physical products that have a regional appeal such as restaurant or food stores selling items of regional flavor, sports companies selling memorabilia for certain college and professional teams, and others. This is also a desirable option if you are offering metropolitan/region services such as tickets to concerts, the theatre, sporting events, etc. These are great markets if you want to start out small with your business and focus on a limited target market before branching out.

Check with your attorney on shipments of certain products into various regions around the world. Wine, for example, is precluded from being shipped into certain U.S. states.

5. Google Local and the Cities Region

Google Local cross checks Yellow Page information with data culled from over 8 billion Web pages to offer search results focused on neighborhood businesses. Use of Google Local is easy; a searcher merely inputs a zip code or a town/city name along with a search term at http://local.google.com

Search Term: Pizza   Zip Code or Location: 38125   Google Search

What is the "Remember this location" check box under the Google Local search? It is simply a way for Google, by depositing a cookie on your computer, to automatically remember your local area of search for future reference so that you do not have to key in the zip code or location each time.

Google does not offer target markets in *every* city of the 240 countries; only major cities outside the United States. This is the most desirable region if you are offering local services such as restaurants, house cleaning services, lawn services, etc.

Here's all you have to do to get your business listed free with Google Local:

How to Add Your Business on Google Local

1. Email an inquiry to: **Local-Listings@Google.com**
2. Google will respond and ask for details about your business
3. Upon response your business will be included in Google Local.

6. The Custom Region

Here Google lets you define a set region from the location of your business or a very specific target market. In this instance you'll have to enter your business address. This target market is defined by a set distance (miles, yards, etc) from your place of business. Think of creating a circle that defines a marketing area around your business or target market. The distance you provide Google is the radius of the circle.

FREE COORDINATE TOOL

TIP: Google offers a free Coordinate Targeting Tool to define your local marketing area under the custom region. See below for details on this high-tech, but easy to use tool.

VI. Google Advertising & Management Tools with Examples

A. Free Google Advertising Tools

Google offers a number of free tools that are very powerful in optimizing your marketing campaign. We will discuss each in detail below.

Five Campaign Management Tools
1. Change Keyword Matching Options 2. Keyword Suggestion Tool 3. Edit Campaign Negative Keywords 4. Conversion Tracking 5. Traffic Estimator

1. Coordinate Targeting Tool

If you do not want a circular area to define the meets and bounds of your local market, Google allows you to define the market by creating any shape using latitude and longitude points (e.g., 35* 20' 31", -120* 5' 42"). The asterisk signifies degrees. This may appear like you'll need to take a navigation class to learn how to do this, but Google once again makes it simple. The following Websites will display latitude and longitude coordinates that you can plug into Google: Maporama.com, Maptools.com and Multimap.com.

In the Custom Region at least 3 latitude and longitude points are required to set the boundaries on your target geographical area. This will create a triangle. If you want to cover a different shaped area such as a rectangle, a fourth point will have to be added. Marketing areas that are separated will require a new AdWords or Image Ads campaign. This may sound expensive, but don't worry. Unlike traditional advertising programs, there is no extra charge from Google for the number of campaigns you set up. You are only limited by your creativity and daily amount that you wish to spend.

Google returns different click-through results for each country and language. This may sound difficult to track, but Google does all the tracking for you.

2. Keyword Suggestion Tool

To help focus your advertising campaign, Google has a tool to more narrowly define your broad search terms. Google provides—free of charge—a powerful Keyword Suggestion Tool to optimize ads for your target market. When you input your broad search term it returns more specific search terms users have used including your broad search term. For each keyword you create, the Keyword Suggestion Tool will return search terms culled from the 20 million searches conducted daily on Google that are variations of your keyword or associated in common searches. This is one of the best tools Google offers and its inner workings will be key to your marketing success. When compiling your ad you'll be asked to input all keywords for which you would like your ad to appear when Google users search on those terms. Then, Google provides a tool that displays search terms users employ that are similar to your own. This often includes common misspellings and alternative queries. Consider:

Keyword	Possible Keyword Suggestion Tool Results
Rice	Basmati Rice Brown Rice Growing Rice Long Grain Rice Long-Grain Rice Longrain Rice Rice-a-Roni Rice Recipes Spanish Rice Sticky Rice Sushi Rice White Rice Wild Rice

3. Traffic Estimator Tool

Google's free Traffic Estimator Tool allows you to get traffic estimates for up to 5000 keywords *before* adding them to your account. This powerful tool will give you an estimated ad position in the AdWords column per keyword based on your maximum CPC and the CTR the keywords are already getting on Google. Before you spend any money on Google it will provide the rating it forecasts for your ad on all keywords you've selected. Adjust your ad *before* you are spending advertising dollars to maximize your ROI.

Traffic Estimator Options

1. Select keywords (keyword=Broad Match; "keyword"=Phrase Match; [keyword]=Exact Match; -keyword=Negative Match);
2. Maximum Cost-Per-Click (CPC) or let Google do it for you, which will return a value with a #1 rank 85% of the time;
3. Select a target language of the 14 available;
4. Select the region (Global/National, Regions and Cities, or Customized); and
5. Select from the list of countries or simply select "All Countries."

Once these options are selected, Google will return your forecast.

Keywords	Clicks/Day	Avg. CPC	Cost/Day	Avg. Position
1970 Mustang	75	$2.87	$452	1.1

This tells us that, on average, competitors in the old car business are paying $2.86 per click on this keyword for the top AdWords position! Use this vital information to map your CPC strategy.

Use the Big 3 in Competitive Data Gathering

1. Competitors within the top positions – Follow URL links within AdWords column;
2. Keywords competitors are bidding on – Use Keyword Estimator Tool as shown above; and
3. How much competitors are paying for keywords – Use combinations of Keyword Estimator and Keyword Suggestion Tools as shown above.

PLACE IN THE TOP 4 POSITIONS FOR BEST RECOGNITION

TIP:

Remember that if a user has their browser set in the "normal view" setting, the number of ads shown in the AdWords column is reduced to only 4 without scrolling. If bidding for the top position is too expensive, reduce the top position CPC amount in the Traffic Estimator to meet your CPC budget and ensure the average position is still 1-4. Keep in mind this is an *average* position estimate. Even the 4th average position may appear in the 2nd spot at times and the 6th at others. Also remember that typically only the top 3 positions are shown in Gmail.

4. Conversion Tracking Tool

Google provides conversion tracking html code that you simply cut and paste into the html code of your Website. The code is placed on the "Thank You" page that appears after a user has purchased from your Website so that Google can track from click to purchase and inform you which keywords are successful in your campaign. Note that Google places the following text "Google Site Stats" on your "Thank You" page to alert users that their purchase has been tracked. Google includes this notification to users as part of its Privacy Policy. The conversion text block itself is customizable to your particular Website.

Two Conversion Tracking Options

1. Pause or Make Active Conversion Tracking
2. Get Conversion Tracking Code - Here Google provides the actual code you copy into the HTML of your Website for this tracking. Follow https://adwords.google.com/select/setup.pdf to view Google's helpful Conversion Tracking Guide, which is in .pdf format.

B. Industry Examples of Advertising Dos and Don'ts

Below are examples of searches covering business-to-business and business-to-consumer markets. In particular, examples are shown for the consumer electronics industry, travel services, real estate services, consumer services, consumer products and the personal services industry, which are common for small businesses. Here we will dissect representative ads in these marketing campaigns and show good and bad advertising practices.

Google Search	Cell Phones

Sponsored Links

Cell phones
Great Free **Phones**. Plans at 29.99
or more with activation.
www.[Website].com

Title exactly matches search term.
Bodylines form one sentence. "Free
Phones" draws attention and starting
monthly plans are priced.

Cell Phones & Plans
Free **Cell** Phone & Free FedEx
T-Mobile, Nextel & Cingular Plans!
www.[Website].com

Title includes search term. Three cell
phone companies listed. "Free cell
Phones" draws attention. Free shipping
listed but no monthly plans.

Free **Cell** Phone
Get cash back & Fast, free shipping
Nokia, Motorola, Samsung & more
[Website].com

Title includes search term and "free"
makes it more compelling than Title of
ad 1 or 2. "Cash back" draws attention.
"Free shipping" listed but no monthly
plans. URL Line is easy to read.

Great **Cell Phones**
The **Phones**, Plans & Prices you want
Only Online. **Cell phones**.
[Website].com

"Great Cell Phones" is less compelling
than the "Free Cell Phone" Title of ad 3.
No prices, plans or phones listed. URL
easy to read/remember.

T- Mobile Special
2 free **phones**, $400 cash rebate
Free accessories & shipping! Aff.
www.[Website].com

Title limited to 1 phone company. "2
free phones" draws attention. "$400
cash rebate" makes ad stand apart from
"cash rebate" alone. "Free accessories
& shipping" is good.

Google defines "affiliate" Websites as those being paid to redirect online visitors to
another Website or distributor. Google requires all affiliates to identify themselves as
such in their ad by using the word "aff." or "(Aff.)." Example:

Cell Phones
Great Free **Phones**. Plans at
$29.99 with activation. (aff.)
[Cell Phone Manufacturer Website].com

Google Search Travel Agency

Sponsored Links

Travel
Book your flight and hotel together
and Save with CoolTravel.
www.[Website].com

> Broad Title. Bodylines flow as one sentence. This ad does little to stand apart. Ands should be replaced with "&."

Spritz Travel Group
Corporate **Travel** Management
Onsites, Booking Tools & Web Fares
www.BottleTreeBooks.com

> Title relies on agency recognition, which searcher may not know. "Corporate Travel Management" would be best in the title. Good capitalization. No punctuation after 1st Bodyline.

Find **Travel** Bargains
Excellent **Travel** Bargains with
us. Search Now & Save!
www.[Website].com

> "Find" not needed in Title. Words such as "Best" and "#1" are better than "Excellent." "Travel Bargains" redundant in Bodyline 2. Good flow of 1st and 2nd Bodylines.

Travel Agency
Your Passport to Savings awaits.
Find Summer Airline Ticket Deals!
[Website].com

> Title matches search term exactly. Good punctuation & capitalization. Ad and services are limited to airline tickets.

Wal-Mart **Travel** Services
Vacation packages, cruises & more
at XYZ. Every Day Low Prices.
[Website].com

> National brand recognized in Title. Bodyline 1 lists a wide range of services. Good sentence flow between Bodylines 1 & 2. URL Line is easily remembered.

Travel Deals -SuperSearch
Search multiple **travel** sites fast!
Find low fares and **travel** deals.
[Website].com

> Title gives a lot of info. Travel search services are clearly identified. Note exclamation point between Bodylines 1 & 2. URL Line is simplified.

> If you want to make claims that your product or service is better than your competitor's, you must have factual data to back up your assertion on the Web page customers first see when clicking on your ad. This could take the form of test data or a performance chart. Avoid Puffery. Comparative or subjective phrases such as "Best," "Cheapest," "Top," or "#1," must be verified on your Website by a third party.

| Google Search | Memphis Real Estate Agents |

Memphis TN Real Estate
Search **Memphis** listings, links to
Germantown-Collierville-attractions
www.[Website].net

> Title is very close to keywords of search.
> Bodylines 1 & 2 flow. Prestigious
> Memphis suburbs listed.

Find a home in **Memphis**
Free - search thousands of homes
for sale in **Memphis** Tennessee
www.[Website].com

> Descriptive Title. "Free" always draws
> attention. Lack of comma between
> "Memphis Tennessee" makes ad look
> sloppy.

Memphis TN Homes
Gain instant online access to
thousands of listings and addresses
www.[Website].com

> Title could be more descriptive. "Instant"
> is a great term to use for busy home
> shoppers. "Thousands" hints at the breadth
> of the site. Term "and addresses" is
> unnecessary.

Find **Real Estate Agents**
Pre-qualified **Real Estate** Agent
in 3 Quick, Easy Steps. Apply Today
www.[Website].com

> Descriptive Title. "Pre-qualified" gives
> credibility. Nice use of capitals. "3 Quick,
> Easy Steps" makes application seem short
> and simple. Nothing in ad linking business
> to Memphis.

Local **Real Estate Agents**
Find a Realtor®, view homes for
sale, foreclosures & mortgage rates
www.[Website].com

> Title better than ad 4. Explains all services.
> Correct use of ® for a registered trademark.
> Bodylines 1 & 2 flow. Nothing in ad
> linking business to Memphis.

Dialer ads are not allowed. Dialers are switching software that change a modem's
dial tone used to access the Internet to a long distance number that is billed to the
Internet user. It comes as no surprise that Google does not permit ads associated with
dialers or dialer software in any way.

Google Search	Incorporate

Sponsored Links

Incorporate Your Business
Incorporate Your Business Online -
Any State. 24/7 Account Access.
www.[Website].com

> Descriptive Title includes search term. Explains services but Bodyline 1 is mostly redundant. "24/7" stands out.

Incorporate
Incorporate in 10 Minutes or Less.
Easy Online Form, Affordable Price.
www.[Website].com

> Title is the exact search term but unused characters could allow it to be more descriptive. Good use of capital letters and punctuation. Themes of quick and cheap done well.

Incorporate for $75
Plus state fee. All 50 states.
Low Fees 1-800-ITS-TIME
www.[Website].com

> Best Title of all five ads because cost is stated. Ad covers it all— incorporation fee, state fee, all 50 states and 1-800 number. Ad does not refer to online service or quick.

Incorporate Your Business
Online For as little $50 plus State
Fees! Fast, Easy & Efficient
www.[Website].com

> Same Title as ad 1 but better since it flows into Bodyline 1. Explains all services. No punctuation at end of Bodyline 2. Good ad that needs to include 1-800 number in this industry.

Low Cost Incs. & LLCs
50 States for U.S. & Int'l Clients
Free Reports, Webcasts 800-462-4633
www.[Website].net

> Only Title that includes "LLCs" & only ad that refers to international clients. No punctuation at end of Bodylines 1 & 2. Nothing in ad that shows registration cost.

Google does not allow AdWords or Image Ads for online gambling. This includes online casinos, sports books, bingo, and affiliates with the primary purpose of driving traffic to online gambling sites.

Google Search	Vitamins

Sponsored Links

The Greatest Vitamin
Top vitamin formulation.
Call 440-773-3591 to order!
www.[Website].com

> Title only pushes one vitamin. What is its name? Bodylines 1 & 2 flow. No cost of vitamin stated. Is it all natural, no artificial ingredients, liquid, etc? 1-800 number would be best.

Vitamin - Up to 75% Off
Name Brand **Vitamins**. Low Prices.
Shop and Save - Buy Now!
www.[Website].com

> "Vitamin" in Title is not bolded because not plural like search term. One letter would have drawn more attention! Name brands & low prices are good. Bodylines 1/2 flow.

Vitamins – Huge Savings
Save 20-50% off over 25,000 items
from over 300 brands every day.
www.[Website].com

> Title includes exact search term & "Huge Savings." Great use of relevant numbers in Bodylines. A large selection of top brands are defined.

Vitamins Megastore
Vitanet offers a large selection of
Name brands at 70% off retail.
http://www.[Website].com

> Title reflects scope of store & includes search term. Bodylines 1 & 2 flow, but "Name" should not be capitalized. Ad 3 much more detailed. URL Line too long; "http://www." not needed.

VitaminLife 20%-70% Off
Discounted prices on 500 brands.
Over 30,000 supplements.
www.[Website].com

> Best ad. Broad search term would be better than trade name in Title. Great use of relevant numbers in Bodylines. Store has more brands, larger selection, & more discounts than ad 3.

> If your ad has a price, special discount, "free," or "giveaway" language, it must be clearly and accurately displayed on your Website within one or two clicks of the page on which customers land after clicking on your ad.

| Google Search | Personal ads |

Sponsored Links

Personal Ads
Online personals & dating made easy
Meet people in chatrooms for free!
www.[Website].com

> Title matches search term exactly. Quick & easy themes made clear. No punctuation at end of Bodyline 1. No mention of cost.

Personal ads
When You're Done with Quantity,
Meet Quality. See our Approach.
www.[Website].com

> Title matches search term exactly. Bodylines flow. No mention of cost. Hints at unique approach to dating.

Personal Ads
Free Sign Up-Browse 1000s Of
Profiles From Singles In Your Area
www.[Website].com

> Best ad of the four. Title matches search term exactly. Bodylines flow. Good use of capitalization. Use of "1000s" makes ad stand out. Local theme is desirable for dating service.

LavaTimes Photo Personals
Create a free profile and see your
dating life heat up. Sign up today!
www.[Website].com

> No incorporation of search term in Title. Only ad that mentions photos, which is very important in the dating arena! Bodylines flow. "Free" profile is good.

C. Prescription Drugs and Related Content

For Websites that seek to advertise online prescription drugs or for those that target prescription drug keywords in the U.S. Country Region, a valid SquareTrade identification number must be provided.

> Only online pharmacies based in the U.S. or Canada may receive a SquareTrade membership. International online pharmacies may not include the U.S. within their Google Country Region.

Here is a link to Google's Online Pharmacy Qualification Program.
Http://www.google.com/adwords/pharmacy_qualification.html.

> If you feel that the Online Pharmacy Qualification Program is not applicable to your Website, you may request an exception.

VII. Overlooked Google Advertising Programs & Management

A. The Froogle Advantage

Since this book is about advertising on Google, it would be remiss without including Google's dedicated shopping site called Froogle (pronounced "Frugal"). Froogle is fast becoming one of the Internet's premier shopping sites. When potential customers search for a product within Froogle, a list of products are shown along with description and pricing information. Thumbnail photos of the product are also included. What's best about Froogle is that it is totally free! That's right. As long as you meet the simple guidelines, there is neither a minimum spending amount nor a charge for clicks. There isn't even a registration fee. Visit www.froogle.com and get your free advertising campaign started today!

> AdWords automatically appear in the right-hand column when users conduct a Froogle search. Froogle is part of Google's Search Network. AdWord clicks within Froogle are charged at the normal click rate that you have specified.

B. Market Your Way to Success Using Google Catalogs

Google provides yet another free way for you to advertise. It's called Google Catalogs. Under this service Google's leading search technology is used on thousands of scanned mail order catalogs. All you have to do to get your product catalog included is to mail it to Google.

How to Add Your Catalog on Google

1. Add Google to your subscriber list;
2. Use this address: **Google Catalogs**
   171 Main Street, #280A
   Los Altos, CA 94022
   USA
3. Send a notification email to: Catalog-Vendors@Google.com once Google is added to your mailing list; and
4. Your catalog will be scanned by Google and placed on its Website within a few days after Google receives it.

C. Zeitgeist Your Way to Increased Sales

Determining what products and services are of interest on the Internet can be difficult for most advertisers. This illusive and ever changing information is essential for a successful Internet marketing campaign. It would take an army of data collection agents to gather this information. Nothing to fear. Google provides yet another free, but relatively little used tool that gathers this information for you. It is called zeitgeist, which is translated "Time Spirit" and can be found at www.google.com/press/zeitgeist.html. Google's Zeitgeist provides the following most popular search category data:

Zeitgeist Popular Search Results

1. Top Image Search Queries
2. Popular TV Shows
3. Popular Text Queries
4. Popular Athletes
5. Popular Men
6. Popular Women
7. Popular Movies
8. Popular Cities
9. Popular Animals
10. Popular News Organizations
11. Popular Airlines
12. Popular Beauty-Related Queries
13. Popular Google News Queries
14. Top Political Queries
15. Top Retailers
16. Top 10 Gaining
17. Top 10 Declining

If you offer travel related services, use the Zeitgeist Popular Cities and Popular Airlines results to target your marketing campaign. If your business is in the multibillion dollar a year cosmetic field, the Zeitgeist Popular Beauty-Related Queries data is a must. There are no limits to how Google's free marketing data can be used.

Google further provides data on the above popular searches in the following countries. Each is hyperlinked for your convenience.

Zeitgeist Countries

1. Australia - www.google.com.au/press/zeitgeist.html
2. Brazil - www.google.com.br/press/zeitgeist.html
3. Canada - www.google.ca/press/zeitgeist.html
4. Denmark - www.google.dk/press/zeitgeist.html
5. Finland - www.google.fi/press/zeitgeist.html
6. France - www.google.fr/press/zeitgeist.html
7. Germany - www.google.de/press/zeitgeist.html
8. Italy - www.google.it/press/zeitgeist.html
9. Japan - www.google.co.jp/press/zeitgeist.html
10. Korea - www.google.co.kr/press/zeitgeist.html
11. Netherlands - www.google.nl/press/zeitgeist.html
12. Russia - www.google.ru/press/zeitgeist.html
13. Spain - www.google.es/press/zeitgeist.html
14. Sweden - www.google.se/press/zeitgeist.html
15. United Kingdom - www.google.co.uk/press/zeitgeist.html
16. United States - www.google.com/press/zeitgeist.html

FINE TUNE YOUR FOREIGN MARKETING CAMPAIGN

TIP: Zeitgeist provides one-year data on the various languages used to access Google. Use this free data to further tailor your marketing campaign such that ads are not only created for various regions but also languages within those regions.

D. Manage Your Google Advertising Campaign Online

We have discussed the most effective ways to start your advertising campaign on Google and how to optimize it so that you gain the most clicks at the lowest cost-Per-Click. Now we will survey the various campaign tools you will encounter inside Google's advertising system. Effective management of these tools and techniques will make your advertising campaign on Google that much more of a success!

Campaign Management		Reports	My Accounts
Campaign Summary| Tools| Conversion Tracking	Search my campaigns:	Google Search

Here is key information you will find on the Campaign Summary page

Campaign Name	Current Status	Current Budget	Clicks	Impr.	CTR	Avg. CPC	Cost	Conv. Rate	Cost/ Conv.
Hammers	Active	$10/day	15	5	2%	$0.10	$1.50	33%	$.50

The above reporting is not in real time. There is a 3-hour buffer so that clicks within this window of time may not be reflected. Google updates campaign summary statistics on a more frequent basis than AdGroup and keyword statistics.

Here is key information you will find on the Tools page under the Campaign Management tab:

Campaign Management		Reports	My Account
Campaign Summary| Tools| Conversion Tracking	Search my campaigns:	Google Search

As discussed above, there are 5 powerful tools Google has provided for your advertising campaign. If you consider the Coordinate Targeting Tool, there are actually 6 tools.

1. Change Keyword Matching Options

1. Apply to:	Hammers

2. Choose match types:

Change all:
Keywords to:

Broad Match	Phrase Match

2. Keyword Tool

Enter one keyword or phrase per line.   Results are tailored to language and country:

All Languages	All Countries
English	United States
Chinese	United Kingdom
(Simplified)	Canada
Chinese	Germany
(Traditional)	
Danish	

3. Edit Campaign Negative Keywords

Add new campaign negative keywords	
Enter words manually... Use this format: -keyword	**...or use Clean Sweep.** Do your negative keywords appear in more than one AdGroup? Remove them from the AdGroup level, and add them at the campaign level.
└^	1. Find negative keywords in <u>all AdGroups</u> └^
<u>Add Keywords</u>	2. Delete from AdGroups and add as campaign negative keywords.

4. Conversion Tracking

*See further details under the Conversion Tracking link below.

5. Traffic Estimator

1. Enter keywords, one per line: |Λ	keyword = broad match [keyword] = exact match "keyword" = phrase match -keyword = negative match	
2. Choose a currency/Max CPC	US Dollars (USD$) |Λ	
	All Languages English Chinese (Simplified) Chinese (Traditional) Danish	O **Global or nationwide** – choose countries O **Regions and cities** – choose states and regions and/or enter cities O **Customized** – enter a radius and address or coordinates	
All Countries United States United Kingdom Canada Germany	**Add >>** **<<Remove**	Selected Countries United States United Kingdom

USE THE AD OPTIMIZATION BUTTON

TIP: The Campaign Summary page includes a check box for ad optimization. By ensuring this box is checked, Google will issue more impressions of your ad for keywords that are getting the most clicks. Likewise, it will slow impressions for key for keywords not receiving many clicks.

This is the key information you will find on the Conversion Tracking page under the Campaign Management tab:

Campaign Management		Reports	My Account
Campaign Summary Tools Conversion Tracking		Search my campaigns:	Google Search

--Here is key information you will find on the Conversion Tracking page under the Reports tab:

Campaign Management	Reports	My Account
Report Center Saved Reports		

Google provides 8 detailed tracking reports that provide views of your advertising campaign from many different angles.

Eight Keyword Reports
1. Keyword Report
2. Ad Text Report
3. Ad Image Report
4. URL Report
5. Account Report
6. Campaign Report
7. AdGroup Report
8. Custom Report

The fields from which you may choose to configure your Keyword Report are as follows:

View	Summary Data |^	
Date Range	Last 7 Days L^ or O [Date Range]	
Campaigns	All Campaigns Hammers	

AdWords Type	All |^	
Keyword Status	Any Status |^	
Keyword Matching	Any Type |^	
Graph	☐ Include Graph of	Avg. CPC |^
Conversions	☐ Show Conversion Stats	
Format	O View Online (Html)	O Downloadable (.csv)
Save & Email	☐ Save This Report as	
	Email it to Me	Never |^

The Keyword Report will look like:

Keyword	Keyword Matching	Keyword Status	AdGroup	Campaign	Max. CPC	Impressions	Clicks	CTR	Avg. CPC	Cost	Avg. Pos.
Sledge Hammers	Phrase	Active	Hammers	Hammers1	$0.10	40	4	10%	$0.08	$0.32	2.4

The fields from which you may pick to configure the Ad Text Report are:

View	Summary Data |^	
Date Range	Last 7 Days L^ or O [Date Range]	
Campaigns	All Campaigns Hammers	

AdWords Type	All |^	
Show Ad	☐ Show Lines of Ad Text	
Graph	☐ Include Graph of	Avg. CPC |^
Conversions	☐ Show Conversion Stats	
Format	○ View Online (Html)	○ Downloadable (.csv)
Save & Email	☐ Save This Report as	
	Email it to Me	Never |^

The Ad Text Report will resemble:

Headline	Description Line 1	Description Line 2	Dest. URL	Display URL	Impr.	Clicks	CTR	Avg. CPC
Sledge Hammer	Phrase	Active	[test].com	Hammer	40	4	10%	$0.08

The fields from which you may choose to configure your Ad Image Report are:

View	Summary Data |^	
Date Range	Last 7 Days L^ or ○ [Date Range]	
Campaigns	All Campaigns Hammers	
Graph	☐ Include Graph of	Avg. CPC |^
Conversions	☐ Show Conversion	

	Stats	
Format	O View Online (Html)	O Downloadable (.csv)
Save & Email	☐ Save This Report as	
	Email it to Me	Never |^

Here are the representative columns the Ad Image Report will generate:

Ad	Ad Name	AdGroup	Campaign	Clicks	CTR	Avg. CPC	Cost
Sledge Hammers 10-20% Off Sledge Hammers. 15 Brands to Choose! [Website].com	Tools 2	Hammers	Hammers1	4	10%	$0.08	$0.32

The fields from which you may choose to configure your URL Report are as follows:

View	Summary Data |^	
Date Range	Last 7 Days ∟^ or O [Date Range]	
Campaigns	All Campaigns Hammers	
AdWords Type	All |^	
Graph	☐ Include Graph of	Avg. CPC |^
Conversions	☐ Show Conversion Stats	
Format	O View Online (Html)	O Downloadable (.csv)
Save & Email	☐ Save This Report as	

	Email it to Me	Never
		|^

Here are the representative columns the URL Report will generate:

Destination URL	AdGroup	Impressions	Clicks	CTR	Avg. CPC	Cost	Avg. Position
[test].com	Hammers	40	4	10%	$0.08	$0.32	2.4

The fields from which you may choose to configure your Account Report are as follows. They are identical to the fields of the URL Report.

View	Summary Data |^	
Date Range	Last 7 Days |^ or O [Date Range]	
Campaigns	All Campaigns Hammers	
AdWords Type	All |^	
Graph	☐ Include Graph of	Avg. CPC |^
Conversions	☐ Show Conversion Stats	
Format	O View Online (Html)	O Downloadable (.csv)
Save & Email	☐ Save This Report as	
	Email it to Me	Never |^

Here are the representative columns the Account Report will generate:

Account	Impressions	Clicks	CTR	Avg. CPC	Cost	Avg. Position
Hammers1	40	4	10%	$0.08	$0.32	2.4

The fields from which you may choose to configure your Campaign Report are:

View	Summary Data |^	
Date Range	Last 7 Days |^ or O [Date Range]	
AdWords Type	All |^	
Campaign Status	Any Status |^	
Graph	☐ Include Graph of	Avg. CPC |^
Conversions	☐ Show Conversion Stats	
Format	O View Online (Html)	O Downloadable (.csv)
Save & Email	☐ Save This Report as	
	Email it to Me	Never |^

Here are the representative columns the Campaign Report will generate:

Campaign	Campaign Status	Impressions	Clicks	CTR	Avg. CPC	Cost	Avg. Position
Hammers	Active	40	4	10%	$0.08	$0.32	2.4

The configure fields for your AdGroup Report are as follows:

View	Summary Data ∣^	
Date Range	Last 7 Days ∣^ or O [Date Range]	
AdWords Type	All ∣^	
AdGroup Status	Any Status ∣^	
Graph	☐ Include Graph of	Avg. CPC ∣^
Conversions	☐ Show Conversion Stats	
Format	O View Online (Html)	O Downloadable (.csv)
Save & Email	☐ Save This Report as	
	Email it to Me	Never ∣^

Here are the representative columns the AdGroup Report will generate:

AdGroup	AdGroup Status	Impressions	Clicks	CTR	Avg. CPC	Cost	Avg. Position
Hammers	Active	40	4	10%	$0.08	$0.32	2.4

USE GOOGLE LINK TO MEASURE YOUR ADVERTISING SUCCESS

TIP: ROI is your best financial measurement of how well your Google advertising campaign is proceeding, but there are other indicators like newsletter opt-ins and building brand identity. Another great measurement is the number of Websites that create links directly to your site. Google easily lets you monitor this by a simple command that is typed in at the search box at Google.com:

| Google Search | Link:[Website].com |

The results shown will be all the Websites that have created a direct hyperlink to your Website. Monitor how the list grows as yet another indication of your Google marketing success that may result in future sales even if you stop advertising!

The fields from which you may choose to configure your Custom Report are numerous. With the Custom Report Google has provided a way to slice and dice your report in almost any fashion.

View	Summary Data |^	
Date Range	Last 7 Days |^ or O [Date Range]	
Detail Level	Click 'Show Options' to further define the level of detail in your reports. Please note that the more selections you make, the longer it will take to run your report. For faster downloads and multiple views, we suggest that you select only necessary fields.	
Values	☐Clicks ☐Cost	

	☐Impressions	☐Maximum CPC
	☐CTR	☐Daily Budget
	☐Avg CPC	☐Avg Position
Ad Text	☐Headline	☐Display URL
	☐Description Line 1	☐Destination URL
	☐ Description Line 2	☐Ad Status
	☐Avg CPC	☐Avg Position
Conversions	☐Conversions	☐Value/Cost
	☐Conversion Rate	☐Value/click
	☐Cost/Conversion	☐Sales(Count & Value)
	☐Transactions Value)	☐Leads (Count &
	☐Cost/Transaction Value)	☐Signups (Count &
	☐Total Value Value)	☐Page Views (Count &
	☐Avg Value Value)	☐Default (Count &
Graph	☐ Include Graph of	Avg. CPC |^
Format	O View Online (Html)	O Downloadable (.csv)
Save & Email	☐ Save This Report as	
	Email it to Me	Never |^

The Custom Report will generate details of your campaign in any of the above categories that you select. The flexibility is in your hands.

AdGroup	AdGroup Status	Impressions	Clicks	CTR	Avg. CPC	Cost	Avg. Position
Hammers	Active	40	4	10%	$0.08	$0.32	2.4

USE GOOGLE ALERTS

TIP: Alerts is another free Google application that tracks keywords on Websites and automatically reports them to you by email. A great way to use this tool is to track your company name as Websites, blogs, etc use it. Google Alerts is a great way to track brand identity and when other Websites have reviewed your product or linked to your Website. Begin your Google Alert tracking today: www.Google.com/alerts?hl=en

There is a third party Website we like better than Google's own alert program. It is found at www.GoogleAlert.com and it is also free. Some of the reasons we like it better are that multiple search results can be tracked. The results also give a *cashed* link that lets you jump right to the part of the Website referring to your product. Surprisingly, GoogleAlert.com also gives you more detailed results than Google itself and tells you the number of total results its tracking for the particular product name or term used.

Campaign Management	Reports	My Account
Report Center Saved Reports		

Under the Saved Reports link, you are able to save each of the 8 reports generated in the Report Center. You can also update your email address for each.

Campaign Management	Reports	My Account
Billing Summary Billing Preferences User Preferences		

Here is key information you will find on the Billing Summary page under the My Account tab:

Month	Date	Activity	Credits	Charges	Balance
June	23rd	Ad Campaign	$40	$4	$36

Campaign Management		Reports	My Account
Billing Summary	Billing Preferences	User Preferences		

Billing Preferences is where you specify the method in which Google will bill you for your ads. When setting up Billing Preferences you are asked the country in which you reside. If, for example, you have an EU billing address, Value Added Tax (VAT) will apply to your ad. Last, you must enter a credit or debit card (American Express, Visa, MasterCard, JCB, and debit cards having a MasterCard or Visa logo only). Google does not accept payment in any other form for your ad campaign.

USE A REWARDS CREDIT CARD

TIP: Using a cash rebate/rewards or frequent flier credit card is a great way to receive perks from advertising on Google along with a possible tax deduction for this business expense! Google will automatically charge your card on a monthly basis and the transaction is paperless.

Campaign Management		Reports	My Account
Billing Summary	Billing Preferences	User Preferences		

Thanks for Reading "Google Advertising A-Z"

BottleTreeBooks.com

Also from BottleTree

OVERTURE & YAHOO ADVERTISING
PLUS 110 TIPS & TRICKS

ISBN: 097625414X

Do you want to learn the ins and outs of Overture and Yahoo advertising to make your products and services available for up to 275 million searches per day? Do you want to take advantage of 110 tips and tricks to dominate selling on Overture and Yahoo? Whether you are new to Pay-Per-Click advertising or a seasoned marketer, *Overture and Yahoo Advertising* will show you how in a quick and easy format loaded with charts, guides, hyperlinks to free Internet advertising tools, tables and 110 tips and tricks to maximizing your Return-on-Investment. See why a successful advertising campaign on Overture and Yahoo is much different than one on Google.

Here is but a sampling of the topics covered:
- ➢ Bid traps – How to exploit and avoid them
- ➢ Get free Overture coupons worth $25 to $50
- ➢ How to get a Premium Listing without bidding in the top 3 spots
- ➢ The Yahoo Premium Listing exception
- ➢ Secrets of Content Match
- ➢ The CNN Premium Listing exception
- ➢ How to list your business for free on Yahoo's Local Match
- ➢ Examples of great ad titles

➢ The best keyword placement within the Bodylines
➢ Definitive ad stylization
➢ Tricks to keyword plurals and misspellings
➢ Guide to Overture foreign countries and languages
➢ 25 examples of ads that work on Yahoo and those that don't
➢ Commonly overlooked Yahoo advertising programs
➢ How to budget and control your monthly spending
➢ And a much more. . .

"Overture & Yahoo Advertising" Table of Contents

III. **Ad Stylization**
   A. Ad Title/Body/URL Lines Overview
      1. Title Line
      2. Bodylines
         a. Use Detached Language
         b. Avoid Keyword Blur
         c. Avoid Superlatives
         d. Display Product Details & Availability
      3. URL Line
   B. Definitive Ad Stylization
      1. Style/Interior Punctuation
      2. Style/Interior Punctuation Continued
      3. Abbreviations/Shorthand/Symbols
      4. Abbreviations/Shorthand/Symbols Continued
      5. Legal Terminology
         a. Content & Precision Match Trademark Usage Guidelines
         b. Local Match Trademark Usage Guidelines
      6. Punctuation & Contractions
      7. Call-to-Action & Generic Words

IV. **Keyword Creation & Management**
   A. Keywords Are Key
   B. Overture's Free Keyword Selector Tool
   C. Why Overture's Free Bid Tool is Vital to Your Success
   D. The Highly Targeted Keywords Campaign
   E. The Keyword Funneling Campaign
   F. Overture's Click Indicator
   G. Keyword Abbreviations, Plurals & Misspellings
   H. Keyword Matching Options
      1. Advanced Match Type
         a. Account Level Advanced Match
         b. Listing Level Advanced Match
      2. Excluded Match Type
      3. Standard Match Type

V. **Overture Ad Positioning, Bid Strategies & Impression**

Frequency
A. The Key to Getting #1 Placement on Overture
B. Bid Gaps
C. Bid Traps - How to Exploit & Prevent Them
D. Why Physical Advertising Space on Yahoo is Important
E. The Amazing Flexibility of Overture
F. How the Time of Day Affects Your CPC

VI. **Foreign Countries & Languages**
A. Use Foreign Countries to Broaden Your Campaign
B. Fast Track Versus Self Serve in the International Marketplace
C. The Amazon Specific Marketing Campaign

VII. **Overture Tracking Tools & Industry Examples of Ads that Work**
A. Free Overture Conversion Tracking & Visitation Tools
    1. Keyword Conversion Counter
    2. URL Tracking
    3. Marketing Console
B. Industry Examples of Crucial Advertising Dos & Don'ts

VIII. **Commonly Overlooked Yahoo Advertising Programs & Management**
A. The Yahoo Shopping Advantage
    1. Yahoo Product Submit
    2. Yahoo Merchant Solutions
    3. Free Crawling of Website
    4. Yahoo Classifieds
B. Buzz Your Way to Increased Sales

IV. **Budgeting & Overture Advertising Campaign Reports**
A. Budgeting Your Monthly Spending
    1. Open Ended Budget
    2. Fixed Budget
    3. Pre-Payment
    4. Manual Budget

B. Direct Traffic Center Report Management
1. Account Activity Detail
2. Account Daily Summary
3. Account Summary
4. Billing Transaction Detail
5. Category Detail
6. Category Summary
7. Intra-Day Account Activity Detail
8. Match Type Activity Detail (25 Terms w/Highest Click Rates)
9. Match Type Activity Detail (25 Terms w/Lowest Click Rates)
10. Monthly Financial Reports
11. Search Term Activity Detail
12. Search Term Summary
13. URL Activity Detail

Sample Section of "Overture & Yahoo Advertising"

Premium Listings

Overture divides its bids into two groups: Those bidding in the top 3 spots are termed Premium Listings and those in the 4-240 bid positions are non-premium listings . . . at least most of the time. We will address the instances when they are Premium Listings below. Premium listings are centered on the page above the search results. Here's an example in Yahoo:

Sponsor Matches	(What are Sponsor Matches)

Coffee with Poe: Historical Novel About Edgar Allan Poe – His life, many romances, beautiful letters and struggles against poverty and the literary community. Live Poe's life from his view.
www.AndrewBarger.com

Horror Poems of Edgar Allan Poe with Definitions – of keywords, phrases and antiquated sayings along with foreign word translations to bring the words of

America's dark poet to life as never before. "The Conqueror Worm," "The Doomed City," "The Raven," and "Ulalume."
www.BottleTreeBooks.com

"The Raven" by Edgar Allan Poe – Read "America's first poem" and view what critics state is one of the world's best poems by the master of horror.
www.[Website].com

THE YAHOO PREMIUM LISTING EXCEPTION

TIP: Yahoo's search results page will commonly display 5 Premium Listings instead of the usual 3, yet there is a big difference between the first 3 listings and the last 2. Here's how it's structured: If you are not in the top 1-3 bid positions, your add will be shown in Premium format at the bottom of the screen *under* the Web search results and as the first 1 and 2 ads in the right-hand column. Try different positions in the top 1-5 bids and see what gets you the most clicks at the lowest cost for your industry.

Overture's Premium Listings are crucial to your advertising campaign. If you cannot afford to bid for top placement on Overture, make sure you bid at least for one of the top 3 spots. Premium Listings appear across the top of the screen for search results on hot Web properties such as Yahoo, Excite and others, and draw much more attention by users. In addition, the top 3 positions are shown on 80% of Overture's network of Websites as opposed to 40% for positions 4 and up. There is also a third advantage to Premium Listings that is just as important. The *entire* ad for the top 3 positions is displayed as opposed to a truncated version. Use one of the top 3 positions to get your full advertising message across to potential purchasers!

Premium Ad (Top 3 Bidders on a Keyword)
Google Advertising A-Z: Essential AdWords and Image Ads tips and tricks to get the most clicks at the lowest cost. Over 60 tips and examples in numerous industries to help you outperform your competition.
www.BottleTreeBooks.com

Non-Premium Ad (4th Bidder and Above)

Google Advertising A-Z
Essential guide to Google
advertising. Over 60 tips . . .
www.BottleTreeBooks.com

*Note how the Non-Premium ad is severely limited in the message it conveys to searchers.

THE CNN PREMIUM LISTING EXCEPTION

TIP: The top 4 listings are shown as Premium ads on CNN.com and Money.CNN.com. If you cannot afford to be one of the top 3 bidders, chose the 4th position. You will get a Premium listing on CNN.com and top spot in the right-hand column for Precision Match ads elsewhere. Another tip for CNN.com is that Premium ads are strictly limited to 5 total lines. Your Title must be limited to 32 total characters or it will take up 2 lines, leaving 1 URL line and only 2 Bodylines to describe your products or services.

a. Premium Listings: Title

Premium Titles are limited to 40 characters, including spaces. This is the only line of the ad where the first letter of each word may be capitalized.

b. Premium Listings: Bodylines

Overture gives advertisers a maximum of 190 characters for Premium Bodylines. Again, this includes all spaces and punctuation.

c. Premium Listings: URL Line

The URL Line in a Premium listing is limited to 255 characters and it must be operational.

DISPLAY YOUR FULL AD

TIP: Premium Listings display your full and complete ad. If you want to get your *entire* advertising message across, a Premium Listing is the way to do it. Overture and its network partners do not truncate any Premium Listing so try to bid for one of the top 3 spots.

OPTIMUM PREMIUM LISTING BID POSITIONING GUIDELINES

1. Bid for one of the top 3 Premium Listing positions;
2. If you cannot afford the top 3 positions, bid the 4th position to ensure ad inclusion on the popular CNN.com Website and a bottom of the page Premium Listing on Yahoo; and
3. At a minimum try to bid for the 5th position to receive a Premium Listing (albeit bottom of the page) on Yahoo.com.

From BottleTree Fiction . . .

ISBN: 1589611047

<u>Coffee with Poe</u> by Andrew Barger is a historical novel that retells Edgar Allan Poe's life as never presented. It's filled with actual letters to his three fiancées, his literary contemporaries (Longfellow, Irving, and Hawthorne), and his bitter enemies. Read about Poe's constant struggles with poverty, love, and acceptance by the literary community. Have a cup of *Coffee with Poe* and live his extraordinary life and mysterious death.

. . . never seen him inspired by any more dangerous stimulant than strong coffee, of which he was very fond & of which [he] drank freely. MacIntosh says that the measure of a man's brain is the amount of coffee he can drink with impunity.

-Sarah Helen Whitman (Mystic, Poet & Poe fiancée), Dec. 13, 1874.

Coffee with Poe - Chapter 1

1811 - Age 2

Frances Allan once again surveyed the folded page of the *Richmond Enquirer*:

Died—On Sunday last, Mrs. Poe, one of the actresses of the company at present playing on the Richmond Boards. By the death of this Lady the Stage has been deprived of one of its chief ornaments. And to say the least of her, she was an interesting Actress, and never failed to catch the applause, and command the admiration, of the beholder.

She turned to her husband. "My heart bursts for the child. Look at him standing there, his tiny hand on her placid forehead. I can think of nothing sweeter."

"This is hardly sweet. The boy's first memories will be the death of his heart two weeks before Christmas." John Allan leaned back and took in the trefoil archways flanking the choir loft and tracery forms of the reticulated stained glass windows. An oaken cross was carved into the pulpit. Amber light lay across the massive organ pipes exposed in the front wall of the sanctuary, their somber noise vibrating the wooden pew on which he sat.

"If it were not for the caseworkers there would only be the boy. He is the lone family member. The Old St. John's Church has never felt so vacant."

"Death invites the company of fools and the greedy," John Allan said.

"Well our motives are of compassion."

I was standing on my tiptoes on a red velvet chair. The flames atop silver candelabras were prancing in the background from drafts seeping through the limestone walls. Helixes of smoke were spiraling toward the rafters. From the Allan's vantagepoint I am convinced they could see the glints of my tears falling into the casket, staining the heavy rouge of my mother's face. I was beside myself in grief.

"Poor child, orphaned in this cruel world at the age of two."

"Do not forget his sister. Rosalie is only a year old," John Allan remarked, straightening his tie. "Thank goodness she is too small to remember this tragic event *or* the loathsome profession of her parents. William Mackenzie and his wife have already adopted her, under blind eye I am sure."

Frances shifted in the pew and pulled the sleeves of her charcoal-gray wool dress to her wrists. Tissues were balled in one hand along with the article. "I would feel more sorrow if the Mackenzies were not a wealthy Richmond family as we are close to becoming. Rosalie will be brought up in the finest of schools and so will Edgar. Thank you for bringing him into the family on my behalf. When do we intend to adopt Edgar? Sooner than later, I hope. Poor, poor child."

"At the moment he has matured into an upstanding citizen of Richmond and is worthy of our good name. Until this time, the boy's upbringing will be my consuming passion. I have given my word to his grandfather."

"You are so rigid."

Ignoring his wife, John Allan remained face forward in his aisle seat, arms crossed.

Frances took one of them. "Edgar's older brother Henry is three and already living with his grandfather. General David Poe and his kind wife will provide the best of homes, but alas not the wealthiest. Obviously the great veteran of the Revolution is unaware his own daughter-in-law is lying cold in her coffin, nary a flower to accompany her to the grave, or he would be present."

"Or perhaps it is because Eliza Poe is a disgrace to the proud family, especially after she led General Poe's son off the road of prosperity."

"Money. Wealth. Is that all you can think of at a time like this? Sacrilege, John. How can you speak of the destitute mother of three young children while she is stiff before us? God have mercy on your soul."

"All I am saying is that General Poe wanted more for his son David than gallivanting around America and Europe acting in third-rate theatrical companies with a commoner. Eliza's last performance was at the Monumental Church. Can you believe such an ... an act in a church?" John shook his head. "Painting the face, dressing in scanty clothes, and practicing the so called arts is not a respectable profession."

"You are nothing but strong headed. I swear if they opened your head they would find an anvil inside."

A caseworker glanced back toward the whispering commotion and frowned. Edgar did not take his eyes off Eliza.

John kept looking forward, jaw muscles popping. Out the side of his mouth, he said, "It is not your place to disrespect, woman."

Frances sighed. She knew her place in his life and it was the size of a postage stamp. "Forgive me, but despite common thinking, poets and playwrights are talen—"

"'Poets and playwrights,'" John interjected, nostrils flaring. "There are no forthright people in the arts. Period."

"And what is Eliza Poe's crime? That of trying to raise her children the best way she knew how? Trying to make a living and then dying of anxiety and exhaustion during the southern leg of her theatrical tour?"

"The crime of this English actress was marrying David Poe, Junior—a promising Baltimore law student—and beguiling him to cast aside an upright profession to join her on stage. It drove the man mad." John backhanded a hymnal slotted in the pew and the clattered was smothered by the music. "Why do you think David Poe deserted his family and died of a drunken stupor a few days ago? The arts made him do it. There is no greater crime than disrespect for profession, self, and family, in that order."

The organ pipes stopped reverberating and a great silence blanketed the sanctuary. With a flip of his tails, the organist was gone behind a carved door. Using both hands, I helped myself down from the velvety chair on which I stood. I stared out into the empty church pews and John Allan motioned me.

For an instant I remained still, a gothic portrait of a toddler in a black coat, knickers, ruffled shirt, and white knee socks. My hair was dark curls. There was a pout on my lips and puffiness around my eyes. I knuckled away the endless tears.

John Allan waved again and a bonnet-wearing caseworker on the front pew compelled me down from the platform.

I stepped off the chair and just stood there for what felt like hours. Chest slumping, my inner reluctance finally gave in to sensibilities. I walked forward, the shiny buckles on my shoes gleaming under the candlelight as I slowly descended the limestone steps. My footfalls echoed off the walls.

Upon stopping next to John Allan I took to surveying my shoe buckles, hands in pockets. John Allan placed a finger under my chin and forced my gaze upward. "Today you begin your new life, Edgar Poe. Today you come to live with me."

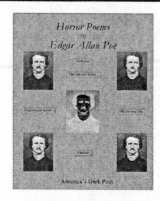

<u>*Horror Poems of Edgar Allan Poe*</u> includes definitions of key words, phrases, and antiquated sayings along with foreign word translations, which bring the words of American's dark poet to life as never before. Within the book are the classic poems: "The Conqueror Worm," "The Doomed City," "The Haunted Palace," "The Raven," and "Ulalume." ISBN: 0976254123

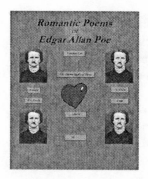

<u>*Romantic Poems of Edgar Allan Poe*</u> also has definitions of key words, phrases, and antiquated sayings along with foreign word translations, which bring the romantic poems of Poe to life. Within the book are the beautiful poems: "Annabel Lee," "The Divine Right of Kings," "Eulalie," "For Annie," "To Helen," "Irene," "Lenore," and "To—." ISBN: 0976254131

BottleTreeBooks.com

Printed in the United States
52147LVS00006B/63